Please remember that this is a library book,
and that it belongs only temporarily to each
person who uses it. Be considerate. Do
not write in this, or any, library book.

The Digital Classroom

HOW TECHNOLOGY IS CHANGING
THE WAY WE TEACH AND LEARN

Edited by David T. Gordon

HARVARD EDUCATION LETTER

Library of Congress Control Number: 00-132449

ISBN 1-883433-07-X

The Harvard Education Letter
Gutman Library Suite 349
6 Appian Way
Cambridge, MA 02138

Cover Design: Alyssa Morris
Group Photograph: Delmy A. Perez
Manuscript Editors: Camille Smith, Amanda Ferguson
Typography: Sheila Walsh

Contents

Teaching and Technology

Managing Technology

Equity and Technology

Looking Ahead

Preface

By David T. Gordon

On my way to the office each morning, I pass the vacant store-front of what used to be an Internet cafe, just off Harvard Square. Above the door a sign reads: "Building Community with Technology." Inside, dust gathers on cafe counters, shadows stretch across bare walls peppered with unused phone jacks.

The cafe is a jarring reminder that although new computer and communications technologies offer unprecedented opportunities for collaboration, we can expect our assumptions about words like "building community" to be tested at every turn. A cafe is a place where people come together to discuss ideas, exchange information, and develop relationships. But does building community in the "dot-com" era still require that people gather in one place, at one time? Is technology itself a compelling enough reason to bring people together?

For those trying to build communities of learners in the digital age, such questions are now part of everyday life. Today's kids are more comfortable with technology than their parents probably ever will be. They surf the Internet, program VCRs, operate cellphones and beepers, scan dozens of cable TV channels in mere seconds, all with dexterity. With both skepticism and awe, we dub them the "Net Generation" or the "Nintendo Generation"—and then we try to figure out what to teach them and how best to do it.

Teachers, parents, school administrators, and students themselves all have the challenging assignment of making sure that these marvelous new resources don't go to waste. Wiring classrooms and purchasing new equipment is just the beginning. Students may perform a web search faster and better than their teachers, but they still need to be taught to filter and critically engage with what they read, see, and hear from the multimedia devices they so deftly operate. And school is still the place where they will need to develop the skills they need to function effectively in the world—to read and write, to add and subtract, to understand how nature and societies are organized and where they fit in. Since school will give most students their first experience in a community where people may be very different from themselves, they'll need to learn how to engage in the kind of constructive collaboration that new technologies permit.

Other questions surface: How can educators tap into the vast resources of the Internet to improve instruction in math, science, literacy, and the humanities? What role will teachers play in a high-tech classroom and what training will they need? How much emphasis on technology is too much? What can be done to bridge the digital divide to ensure an equitable education for all?

The authors of *The Digital Classroom* highlight real people and programs that deal with the exhilarating, baffling changes brought about by new technologies. In keeping with the mission of the *Harvard Education Letter* to serve as a bridge between research and practice, *The Digital Classroom* highlights the innovative work of education scholars and practitioners in a matter-of-fact, jargon-free way.

Though it does not pretend to provide all the answers, this book adds varied and informed perspectives to the ongoing conversation about the best uses of educational technology. We have included information on the programs, experts, books, reports, and articles for each topic in our "For Further Information" sections. We encourage you to use these resources—as well as the remarkable new technologies described in this book—to help build better communities of learning.

Special thanks are owed to Kelly Graves-Desai, editorial director of the *Harvard Education Letter*, for her enthusiasm, wisdom, and commitment to excellence. This project would not have happened without her. Also, thanks to our Editorial Advisory Board for reading and commenting on the chapters. Marya Levenson, Catherine Snow, Douglas Winsor, and faculty editor Richard F. Elmore provided many helpful suggestions.

Karen E. Maloney, director of the Harvard Education Publishing Group, gave her support and many important suggestions. Izumi Doi provided invaluable research assistance, and production editor Dody Riggs offered what she always does: superb, no-nonsense counsel and an expert eye for detail.

Finally, I am especially grateful to Andrea Oseas, assistant director of the Technology in Education program at Harvard's Graduate School of Education, for so generously sharing her time, advice, and insights. Her contribution was essential.

The Digital Classroom

Introduction:
An Invitation to Ask
"What if . . . ?"

By Andrea Oseas

These days very few people in the educational field are neutral about technology. Buoyed by mass media's obsession with the Internet, it has fast become a partisan issue, arousing passions usually reserved for matters of intense controversy, like anchovies or capital punishment. But whether digital technology is met with unbridled enthusiasm or fear and loathing, the tenor of our conversations has changed dramatically. The Information Revolution is under way, as irreversible as the Industrial Revolution and every bit as momentous.

Whether or not we choose to be, we are actors in the drama of technological progress. As the Internet takes up residence in our offices, homes, and schools, we no longer have the prerogative to view technology as optional. The world in which children (and, by extension, parents and teachers) grow, learn, and interact will have significantly different modes of exchange than those of the previous generation. Developments driven by a global economy have experts and prognosticators predicting that the prevailing currency will be information. Lucky for us the distribution of information is a relatively inexpensive enterprise, creating the opportunity to spread some of the wealth traditionally confined to economically privileged populations.

The progressive potential of new digital technologies can boggle the mind, but, for obvious reasons, the dividends of progress will not be deposited automatically into the accounts of the most needy, not unless we and others are committed to this outcome. On the other side of the coin, the Internet is a fundamental contributor to an ever-growing information glut that requires the ability to discriminate between fact and fiction, waste and value, that all too few possess.

And this is precisely where that rare bird, the technology-savvy teacher, comes in. Educational technologies are likely to have little impact on students' ability to learn without trained teachers to guide and frame their use. And we cannot foster in our students the ability to think creatively and analytically about how to navigate their way through this boundless sea of information if we haven't appropriately trained our teachers to do so first. We need to focus our attention and resources on those who will mediate between learning tools and understanding. Information may be free, but learning to synthesize it into meaning comes at a cost of time and expertise, which we now recognize as the axis of the digital divide.

And thus we must tackle the exigencies of budgetary constraints. We know, for instance, that thoughtfully implemented technology is capable of reinvigorating the ecology of learning environments. But how many of us are prepared to decide what to sacrifice in the equation? Art? Music? Sports? The hard task for contemporary strategists and policy makers is defining just which objectives we aim to achieve. Higher test scores? Improved literacy? Job readiness? Material prosperity? Whose agenda will be advanced? Whose model of reform? Reflection upon these and related questions is not so much a luxury as a responsibility, because technology can be as powerful a tool in the hands of fools as in the hands of the wise.

Making Sense of Chaos

So how do we begin making sense out of the chaos of information at our fingertips? First, listen to the neo-Luddites when they remind us of the hidden costs of any innovation. Our infatuation with technology, they insist, will lead to the destabilization of our most cherished civic and cultural mainstays. They could be right; they've been right before. Television promotes numbed inertia as it floods viewers with images of gratuitous violence and material excess; robots replace blue-collar jobs without provisions made for adequate restitution to dispatched workers; computers broaden the chasm between the haves and the have-nots, strengthening the status quo of the privileged, often at the expense of the poor. Historians know that every new technology has unexpected consequences as well as predictable ones that are overlooked in the early stages of promotion. Humans, after all, do have a rather shabby record when it comes to reflecting on new innovations before adopting them wholesale.

Then listen to the technological enthusiasts as they evangelize new digital advances, describing unprecedented ways to solve old and new problems alike. The Web's capacity for collaboration offers new models for learning and meaning making as well as the potential for cross-cultural partnerships never before possible. Many educational technologies adapt easily to support different learning styles, helping non-traditional learners earn a seat at the achievement table. Debate as we may the technocratic notion of progress, it *is* bolstered with ample evidence. Consider improvements that have sprung from technological innovations like the printing press (often cited as the mainspring of the Reformation) and vaccinations. Consider life without newspapers, radio, and *Sesame Street*. Or life without the computers that drive our microwaves, clock radios, and VCRs. Ask users of assistive technology how their lives have been enhanced and you're certain to hear passionate testimonials.

And then, after you've listened and thought carefully about these issues, and read as much as you can from researchers and practitioners in the field, begin envisioning which of our ideals could be served. For instance, how we can harness the potential of technology toward the goals of educational equity and reform, cultural enrichment and the fulfillment of democratic principles? What is of lasting value and what should be discarded? What amazing feats can we accomplish now, for the first time, with these new tools?

What Was, Is, Can Be

The Digital Classroom offers an examination of many of the critical issues facing educators, policy makers, and parents today. From the cognitive impact of early immersion in technology to the broader cultural implications of distributed learning, scholars and practitioners are exploring and reflecting on the role of technology in learning contexts. Included in this collection are articles and essays that address the changing notions of teaching and learning in the digital age; an analysis of what was, is, and can be. Assistance for those sorting through ways that technology can strengthen what is known to work and redress that which doesn't can be found in this anthology.

The continuing presence of rapidly evolving technology is a given. Rushing headlong into the digital age need not be a passive experience, however. Deciding how information technology is used, in ways inspiring or retrogressive, is, to some extent, up to us. Change has its own momentum, but we can help plot its trajectory. While the temptation exists to use digital tools to buttress what is already known about the ways that people learn, there are likely to be shifts in pedagogical theory and practice to consider as we make headway in these uncharted waters. The classroom of today is undergoing a radical transformation, and, as responsible citizens, we need to roll up our sleeves and contribute, in any way that we can, to the conceptualization of learning environments that reflect our hopes, dreams, and values in a changing world.

The authors of *The Digital Classroom* extend to all an invitation to stretch our critical faculties, reevaluate our practices and conventions, and spend some time pondering "What if . . . ?"—the origin of all great ideas. Although we may not be able to predict the future, we can, if we choose, participate in its construction.

Myths and Realities about Technology in K-12 Schools

Only a clear-eyed commitment to central educational goals will get us a substantial return on our investment

By Glenn M. Kleiman

We are in the midst of an explosion of multimedia digital technology—computers and all that goes with them—in K-12 schools throughout the country. Propelled by federal, state, and local initiatives, schools spent an estimated $6.9 billion in 1999 on desktop computers, servers, routers, wiring, Internet access, software, and everything else involved in making modern technology available. Education funds are enhancing the bottom lines of Intel, Microsoft, Apple, Cisco, IBM, and other high-tech companies.

But will we receive an adequate return on investment to the *educational bottom line*? That is, will all this technology improve education for large numbers of students? Will it make our educational systems more effective and efficient? Will it help schools better prepare students for their lives in the 21st century?

As we begin this new century, the investment in technology for schools resembles the investments being made in many "dot-com" Internet companies. In both cases, the investments are based on the *potential* of new technologies, in the hope that this potential will be fulfilled in the coming years. And in both cases the investments involve significant risks and may be a long way from yielding adequate returns.

Maximizing our investment in technology requires a clear vision of our goals and well-developed plans for achieving them. Unfortunately, the rapid influx of technology into schools is, in many cases, running ahead of the educational vision and careful planning necessary to put technology to good use. In fact, what is being done is often based on misconceptions or myths about what is required to gain substantial educational returns.

Myth #1: Putting computers into schools will directly improve learning; more computers will result in greater improvements.

Computers are powerful and flexible tools that can enhance teaching and learning in innumerable ways. However, the value of a computer, like that of any tool, depends upon what purposes it serves and how well it is used. Computers can be used in positive ways—such as to help make learning more engaging, to better address the needs of individual students, to provide access to a wealth of information, and to encourage students to explore and create; or in negative ways—such as to play mindless games, access inappropriate materials, or isolate students.

Many computers in schools, even up-to-date multimedia computers with high-speed Internet access, are not being used in ways that significantly enhance teaching and learning. There are many reasons for this, including the following:

- Teachers have not received adequate training and support for integrating technology into the core of day-to-day classroom instruction, so computers are used around the edges of the class's main work—for example, to reward students who complete their work quickly, to provide drills for students who are struggling with specific skills, or for occasional special activities. While these uses are beneficial, they don't justify the size of the investment.
- Teachers often don't have software that supports major curriculum goals, is consistent with their approaches to teaching, and is well designed for classroom use. While much good educational software has been developed, finding and obtaining what you need to run on the computers you have that also fits into your curriculum often remains difficult.
- Technical support is often insufficient, so that if a computer problem occurs that the teacher and students cannot solve, there may be long delays before a technician is available to address it. Thus teachers feel they cannot depend upon the technology, so they do not plan to use it for important purposes in the classroom.
- The ways computers are made available are often inconsistent with teachers' approaches to curriculum planning and classroom management. Many schools have been placing computers in every classroom, aiming for a ratio of one computer for every six students. This requires teachers to organize daily activities so that some stu-

dents can be working on the computers while others are engaged in other tasks—a style of classroom management that may be new to many teachers, especially above the elementary level. In schools without computers in the classrooms, teachers have to move the class to a computer lab, which must be scheduled well in advance. Since this situation makes it difficult to integrate computers into the flow of lessons, it often encourages teachers to treat computer activities as special events, rather than as central to the curriculum.

• In developing curriculum materials, publishers have not been able to assume that schools have sufficient computers or teacher expertise to make use of technology central to the curriculum. Therefore, they have typically included computer activities only as optional supplements to other class work.

The reality corresponding to Myth #1 is that all this expensive technology will yield little educational return until schools and districts address the need for professional development, technical support, the availability of appropriate software, classroom management, and curriculum integration.

Myth #2: There are agreed-upon goals and "best practices" that define how computers should be used in K-12 classrooms.

What educational purposes should computers serve in the classroom? When we explore this key question, we often find many different implicit views within a school or district. Unless these views are articulated and clarified and a consensus is reached, the diverging views can lead to conflicting expectations, approaches to implementing technology, and criteria for evaluating its impact, all of which can create barriers to moving forward effectively. The most common goals for using technology in schools include the following:

• Improve students' acquisition of basic math, reading, and writing skills, and their content knowledge in specific subject areas, which will lead to higher scores on standardized tests. This goal often leads to the use of drill-and-practice programs, integrated-learning systems (which provide online lessons and quizzes, adjusting the pace of lessons for each student), and software adjuncts to textbooks.

- Motivate students. This goal is often based on the view that schools need to use multimedia, visually rich materials that capture the interest of students. In addition, technology can help teachers provide multiple paths to learning to fit individual students' learning styles and strengths. It can enable students to work with greater autonomy, collaborate with peers and mentors, and gain access to more information related to their own interests, all of which can help engage their interest.

- Broaden curriculum objectives, adding more problem-solving, inquiry, project-based learning, and collaborative work. This goal often leads to students' using simulations, searching for information on the Web, and preparing reports and presentations using word processors, databases, computer graphic tools, and multimedia presentation software.

- Enable teachers to strengthen their own preferred approaches. For example, a science teacher who primarily lectures may use a computer and a large display to provide visual support for the lectures, while another teacher who favors a more inquiry-based approach may add simulations and experiments with computer-based measuring devices and analysis software.

- Better prepare students for the workplace. This goal often leads schools to add a technology strand to the curriculum, so that students learn keyboarding, basic computer operations, and standard applications such as word processors and databases. However, this does not address the major needs articulated by business leaders, who are concerned that their job applicants have strong skills in literacy, numeracy, and problem-solving; know how to gather, organize, and analyze information; communicate well; work successfully in collaborative teams; and be able to learn effectively.

- Update education for the 21st century. Many believe that our changing world requires that we reconsider the very structure and culture of our schools and our classrooms, along with what we teach and how we teach it. Visions of the future vary widely, but most feature increased student autonomy, more collaborative work both face to face and online, more global connections, richer learning resources than traditional textbooks, and more inquiry, interdisciplinary, and project-based learning.

Of course, a school district may strive to meet more than one of these goals at the same time. But each goal selected will make demands upon resources—human as well as technological—and will lead to certain strategies for implementing and supporting the uses of technology. And, most important, different goals will lead to different criteria for evaluating whether the technology is used successfully.

So the reality corresponding to Myth #2 is that educational goals must be clarified and that plans for purchasing, using, and evaluating the impact of technology must be developed to fit those goals. We don't want the cart filled with computer hardware to be leading the educational horse.

Myth #3: Once teachers learn the basics of using a computer, they are ready to put the technology to effective use.

Technology can affect what needs to be taught, how it can be taught, how classrooms are organized and managed, and the roles and expectations of both teachers and students. That is, a technology-enhanced classroom may have both different goals and a somewhat different culture from a traditional classroom.

A long-term study of the Apple Classroom of Tomorrow (ACOT) project followed teachers over several years as they learned to use technology in their classrooms (with lots of computers, software, professional development, and support available). The researchers identified five stages of "instructional evolution" for using technology:

1. At the *entry* stage, teachers experience both trepidation and excitement as they learn to master the new tools themselves and begin to plan how to use them in their classrooms. They are often concerned about the time and effort required and wonder whether computers will ever be effective learning tools in their classrooms.
2. At the *adoption* stage, teachers begin to blend technology into their classroom practices, without making any significant changes to those practices. They may, for example, have students use drill-and-practice programs or word processors—tools that may fit easily into the current curriculum.
3. At the *adaptation* stage, the new technology becomes thoroughly integrated into traditional classroom practices. Word processors, data-

bases, graphic programs, presentation tools, and content-specific software are used frequently. At this stage, teachers typically begin to see some real benefits, finding that students learn more, produce better work, and are more engaged in learning.

4. At the *appropriation* stage, the teachers understand technology and use it effortlessly in their own work and in the classroom. By now the teachers have difficulty imagining how they would function without computers.

5. At the *invention* stage, teachers are ready to experiment with new instructional patterns and ways of relating to students and to other teachers. Interdisciplinary project-based instruction, team teaching, and individually paced instruction become common. In the ACOT study, students of teachers at this stage began to show high levels of skill with technology, an ability to learn on their own, problem-solving skills, and more collaborative work patterns.

The ACOT study also documents the types of training and support that teachers need as they advance through these levels. Clearly, a basic introduction to computers supports only the first stage of this multi-year evolution.

The reality corresponding to Myth #3 is that for technology to be used fully in K-12 schools, significant changes are required in teaching practices, curriculum, and classroom organization; that these changes take place over years, not weeks or months, and require significant professional development and support for teachers; and that the needed levels of training and support change as teachers progress through these stages.

Myth #4: The typical district technology plan is sufficient for putting technology to effective use.

Almost every school district has a technology plan in place, often developed as a requirement to be eligible for federal or state funding. Typically, these plans specify a three- to five-year vision of what hardware, software, and networking capability will be purchased, along with some planning about teacher training, technical support and maintenance, acceptable use policies, and budgeting. Some plans also address integrating technology into the curriculum, evaluating the impact of technology on teaching and learning, and reviewing and updating the plan, but, unfortunately, these critical elements often receive only cursory attention.

Technology plans tend to turn technology into a goal in and of itself, and to separate it from other educational goals and plans. But technology is a tool, and technology planning is like planning for the purchase and use of construction tools—the first step is to design the structure to be built.

The reality corresponding to Myth #4 is that to use technology effectively we must fully integrate it into school improvement plans, special education plans, curriculum plans, professional development plans, and all the other plans formulated by schools and districts. Significant educational returns require that technology be viewed as providing tools to meet central educational goals, not as defining a new, separate set of goals.

Myth #5: Equity can be achieved by ensuring that schools in poor communities have the same student-to-computer ratios as schools in wealthier communities.

The federal E-rate program and many others have helped schools in inner-city and poor rural communities purchase computers and Internet access, with the goal of reducing what is often called the "digital divide"—the gap between "information haves and have-nots." Making the technology available is only a first step. Recent studies have documented that teachers in poor inner-city and rural schools have significantly less training to use technology than teachers in wealthier schools, that technical support systems are not as well funded, and that the uses of computers in the classroom tend to be very different. Students in underserved communities are more likely to use computers for drill-and-practice and integrated-learning system lessons, while students in other communities are more likely to use computers to support inquiry-based, project-based, and collaborative learning. The difference is very significant: for the first group, the computer is in control and leads the students through the lessons, while in the second group the students are controlling computers for their own purposes.

The reality corresponding to Myth #5 is that when considering issues of equity we need to examine all the essential conditions for making computers into effective teaching and learning tools, not just the number of computers purchased.

The central theme underlying all these myths is that while modern technology has great potential to enhance teaching and learning, turning that potential into reality on a large scale is a complex, multifaceted task. The key determinant of our success will not be the number of computers purchased or cables installed, but rather how we define educational visions, prepare and support teachers, design curriculum, address issues of equity, and respond to the rapidly changing world. As is always the case in efforts to improve K-12 education, simple, short-term solutions turn out to be illusions; long-term, carefully planned commitments are required.

For Further Information

Taking TCO to the Classroom: A School Administrator's Guide to Planning for the Total Cost of New Technology. The Consortium for School Networking, 1555 Connecticut Ave., N.W., Suite 200, Washington, DC 20036; tel: 202-466-6296; fax: 202-462-9043. **www.cosn.org/tco**

"High-Tech Pathways to Better Schools." In *Education Week*'s special report, "Technology Counts '98," October 1, 1998. **www.edweek.org/sreports/tc98/cs/cs-n.htm**

D. Harrington-Lueker. "Technology Works Best When It Serves Clear Educational Goals." *Harvard Education Letter* 13, no. 6 (November/December 1997): 1–5. **www.edletter. org/past/issues/1997-nd/technology.shtml**

J. Hawkins, R. Spielvogel, and E. Marks Panush. *National Study Tour of District Technology Integration: Summary Report.* New York: EDC/Center for Children and Technology Report No. 14, 1996. **www.edc.org/LNT/news/Issue4/cct14pdf.htm**

M. Honey, K. McMillan Culp, and F. Carrigg. *Perspectives on Technology and Education Research: Lessons from the Past and Present.* Washington, DC: U.S. Department of Education, Secretary's Conference on Educational Technology, June 1999. **www.ed.gov/ Technology/TechConf/1999/whitepapers/paper1.html**

G. Kleiman and K. Johnson. "Professional Development: From Reports to Reality." *Leadership and the New Technologies Perspectives* (online journal).
Part 1, September 1998: **www.edc.org/LNT/news/Issue5/feature.htm**
Part 2, November 1998: **www.edc.org/LNT/news/Issue6/feature.htm**

Technology in American Schools: Seven Dimensions for Gauging Progress—A Policymaker's Guide. Santa Monica, CA: Milken Exchange on Education Technology, 1998. **www.milkenexchange.org/policy/sevendimensions.pdf**

R.J. Murnane and F. Levy. *Teaching the New Basic Skills: Principles for Educating Children to Thrive in a Changing Economy.* New York: Free Press, 1996.

S. Rockman. *Leader's Guide to Education Technology.* Available online via the National School Board Foundation's EDvancenet web site. To order a printed copy, call 800-706-6722 and request item #03-144-W. **www.edvancenet.org/res_guide_pdf.shtml**

J.H. Sandholtz, C. Rignstaff, and D.C. Dwyer. *Teaching with Technology: Creating Student-Centered Classrooms.* New York: Teachers College Press, 1997.

SouthEast and Islands Regional Technology in Education Consortium. *Factors That Affect the Effective Use of Technology for Teaching and Learning: Lessons Learned from the SEIR-TEC Intensive Site Schools.* Greensboro, NC: SEIR-TEC, 1998. **www.seirtec. org/publications/lessons.html**

P. Starr. "Computing Our Way to Educational Reform." *American Prospect* 27 (July-August 1996): 50–60. **http://prospect.org/archives/27/27star.html**

Learning and Technology

High-Tech Kids: Trailblazers or Guinea Pigs?

Some educators warn that too much computer use might do more harm than good—especially for very young students

By Joan Westreich

Agroup of student archaeologists at Til Barsip, an ancient Assyrian site in what is now Syria, carefully excavates statuary, urns, and other artifacts. The young explorers measure, weigh, and record each discovery. Attempting to understand their finds in historical, social, and religious contexts, the students make inferences and develop hypotheses about the significance of the excavated material after rounds of debate with fellow team members.

They buttress their arguments using research culled from a worldwide network of library, museum, and university collections, as well as databases such as Perseus and Voyager's Louvre videodisk. After further debate, the students revise their hypotheses. As each new artifact is unearthed, the cycle repeats—and a cognitive shift occurs in the students' construction of history.

The best part of the exercise is that the young explorers never leave their sixth-grade classrooms at The Dalton School, an independent K-12 school in New York City. They are engaged in a popular grade-wide project that has been a fixture at Dalton for the past dozen years. Archaeotype, a computerized archaeological simulation, enables students to transcend the physical constraints of the classroom during the 11-week "virtual dig."

Developed by Dalton's resident archaeologist Neil J. Goldberg, history teacher Mary Kate Brown, and technologist William Waldman, Archaeotype is described by its creators as a "network-based multimedia alternative to the textbook-bound sixth-grade curriculum in the Ancient World." The innovative program, according to Goldberg, "encourages analytic, research, and expository writing skills."

Because of the sheer scale of the virtual site, students must work collaboratively throughout all stages of the process—ultimately producing a final document of their findings. Roles shift. Teachers are no longer "glorified storytellers; they become guides," says Goldberg. One of the critical tasks of the teacher-guides is to locate and annotate worthwhile articles and other research material. While acknowledging that teachers may find themselves "physically exhausted" in so dynamic a learning environment, Goldberg says teachers also discover that they "are engaging with students in a way they never did before."

As the teachers' stance shifts, so does that of the students. The young explorers and experimenters no longer sit back and passively absorb canonized information. They learn to embrace ambiguity as they compare their team's findings with those of other teams. Adding to a database compiled by students in previous years, they come to understand, Goldberg reports, that history is, after all, "an interpretation."

Archaeotype is just one example of The Dalton School's successful integration of technology into the classroom, a process that begins in kindergarten. Clearly, Dalton is an example of a best-case scenario and does not reflect the norm. How many schools in the United States can claim a staff archaeologist, not to mention 11 full-time professionals who provide curriculum development and software support to teachers and students?

Educational technology is proving to be an exciting and effective way of giving students of all abilities and backgrounds more educational opportunity. There is sufficient data to show that "when it is used well, technology can have a marked effect in improving children's learning," according to Chris Dede, professor of education and information technology at George Mason University and a technology consultant to the U.S. Department of Education.

For instance, assistive or remedial technology may permit a child with cerebral palsy to move a cursor with her eyes, or provide an autistic child for whom face-to-face contact is difficult with a safe way to communicate. Connie Smith, principal of the K-6 Juarez-Lincoln Accelerated School in San Diego, finds educational technology to be a "democratizing tool" for her economically disadvantaged students. In a school where 17 languages are spoken, computers allow children to work at their own pace. "The computer is patient, the cursor will wait, and you can go as fast or as slowly as you need to go," says Smith.

David Cavallo, a computer scientist and researcher at the Massachusetts Institute of Technology, is witnessing the democratizing effect of computers in a project at a juvenile jail in Maine. Drawing on the work of his MIT colleague Seymour Papert, who developed the innovative LOGO programming language, Cavallo helps children build their own computer games and work with robotics. These activities, he reports, have "opened up pathways to work in science and mathematics" for some students who had been "non-readers and non-writers."

Educational psychologist Jane Healy applauds programs like Archae-otype, which accommodate multiple learning styles and promote analyt-ical skills and problem-solving. In her 1998 book, *Failure to Connect: How Computers Affect Our Children's Minds—For Better and Worse*, Healy cites numerous examples of developmentally appropriate, curric-ulum-supportive, and cost-effective programs and software that are used in the classroom.

Critics—many of whom are classroom teachers—favor doing more research before allocating scarce educational dollars to technology.

At the same time, she raises concerns about what she views as the na-tion's headlong rush to acquire technology in schools. In this Healy is not alone. She and other critics—many of whom are classroom teach-ers—favor proceeding more slowly and doing more research before allo-cating scarce educational dollars to technology.

Healy believes we need to ask more questions about the impact of ed-ucational technology on children—"questions about what computers are doing to children's brains, social health, and physical health. Con-cerned parents and educators must demand research to get these an-swers," she adds. She also recommends asking questions about cost-effectiveness, educational value, teacher training, and curriculum and technology support.

Developmental issues are high on Healy's list of priorities. She takes a firm stance against computer use by children before the age of seven, when they develop the capacity to think symbolically instead of only concretely: "Up to that time, I think it is doubtful that normally develop-ing children need computers. They may be more harmed than helped."

At least with respect to educational technology's effects on the brain, Chris Dede of George Mason University would agree. He observes: "It is difficult to know what kind of brain studies could be done that would yield conclusive findings. From a common-sense point of view, we know that children need a lot of experiences and stimulation for their nervous systems to develop, so it would be a mistake to favor virtual stimulation."

Drawing on her own and other psychologists' clinical experience, Healy faults much of the classroom technology she has seen: "Age-appropriate computer use may help establish some forms of [brain] connections, but inappropriate use may also build resistant habits that interfere with academic learning. Once set into the brain's connectivity, such patterns are hard to break." This conviction fuels Healy's argument against children using computers before age seven.

In an interview with the *Harvard Education Letter,* Healy framed her concerns about the prevalence of game-like software this way: "It is done too quickly, without language, thought, or much envisioning on the part of children." These types of experiences "empty their minds of the attributes that make people imaginative, creative, and thoughtful." In addition, with many applications, children are "reduced to the level of tools of the machine, learning to punch buttons as fast as they can to get a nice reward."

Healy wonders whether frequent use of such software will have an impact on children's "ability to conceptualize and their motivation to do independent problem-solving that doesn't have an immediate reward attached and that requires some mental effort."

Healy raises other serious concerns as well. Some teachers report that their students are experiencing headaches, vision problems, and carpal tunnel syndrome or "video wrist." And unanswered questions remain about electromagnetic radiation with some computers. "[That] we've barely addressed these issues," says Healy, "indicates to me that we are using this generation of children as guinea pigs."

Educators such as James Lerman of The Dalton School disagree with this assessment. A longtime teacher and staff developer, Lerman is the school's director of technology in the New Lab for Teaching and Learning. "We view technology as another arrow in our quiver," he says. "We don't teach technology for its own sake. We see it as useful to the extent that it supports teaching and learning. In kindergarten, it is as concrete an experience as possible."

Lerman notes that children learn how to use computers and engage in structured activities in which they gain facility using the mouse and navigating programs. "They do some drawing and participate in language arts activities that will help them understand the relationship between the written, read, and spoken word." The youngsters learn that they can make the computer do things. In other words, they become active participants in their environment, not passive observers.

One of the few structured computer experiences at Dalton takes place in fourth grade, when students are taught keyboarding—"an important skill that one needs in order to take maximum advantage of technology." By this age, the students have made the transition to formal operations and are capable of making abstract connections between symbol systems and thought processes. "Teaching and learning become more abstract and more oriented toward books, and teachers are encouraged to make use of technology in the ways that make the best sense to them," Lerman explains.

Making Tough Decisions

Besides developmental and health issues, Healy and her fellow techno-skeptics raise questions about the allocation of educational resources. Each year, some $5 billion is spent in the United States on classroom computers alone. Critics argue that a portion of these funds would be better spent preserving traditional music, art, and remediation programs, reducing class size, and improving teacher training. Many of these critics assert that expenditures for lower-tech solutions may also represent better educational decisions. "What can this technology do that can't be achieved better through human means or a less expensive means?" asks Healy. "The question we should be asking is which technology can deliver this particular aspect of learning best."

Stanford University education professor Larry Cuban takes a similar approach. At a recent conference, Cuban observed that addressing cost-effectiveness forces those who seek funding "to consider alternatives that have been overshadowed by the hype over classroom technologies." No responsible educator or administrator sets out to squander limited resources or to be insensitive to the developmental or physical needs of children. But when they turn to the existing research studies for guidance, they are confronted with inconclusive and conflicting data. Andrea

Oseas, assistant director of Harvard's Educational Technology Center (ETC), acknowledges that "in a field that is changing daily, the research is fundamentally anecdotal."

According to Cathleen Norris and Jennifer Smolka of the University of North Texas College of Education and Elliot Soloway of University of Michigan's School of Education, who analyzed 60 empirical studies on using computers to teach writing, "Research articles are written, by and large, for other researchers; their style of reporting does not address the question, 'What can a teacher learn from this study that is applicable to their classroom today?'" To remedy "major lapses and gaps in the research literature," they recommend that researchers collaborate with teachers, curriculum developers, psychologists, and other professionals who work with children to find out what information is truly useful for practitioners.

This is the approach taken at ETC, whose goal of improving educational practice in science, mathematics, and computing has led to collaborative research projects with four Massachusetts school districts. Experienced teachers are part of every research group. A recent ETC report notes: "The views of school people inform every stage of the work so that our research addresses their central concerns, our findings are interpreted in light of their experience, and our lessons are designed to be compatible with their values and to blend readily with existing instruction."

The Milken Exchange on Education Technology, a clearinghouse for research and information on learning technology, has sponsored many studies. In 1999 it assembled summaries of the five largest studies of educational technology under the title *The Impact of Education Technology on Student Achievement: What the Most Current Research Has to Say*. One highlight is James Kulik's 1994 meta-analysis of more than 500 studies of students in elementary schools through college. Kulik's findings were rather modest: "On average, students who used computer-based instruction scored at the 64th percentile on tests of achievement compared to students in the control conditions without computers, who scored at the 50th percentile; students learn more in less time when they receive computer-based instruction; and students like their classes more and develop more positive attitudes when their classes include computer-based instruction."

In *Failure to Connect,* Healy cautions against "overly eager interpretation" of the "lukewarm results" of recent meta-studies, many of which, she says, have been conducted by researchers or organizations that stand to benefit financially from the use of educational technology:

> We still await research telling us how—or even whether—software can best be used to teach either subject matter or skills. Four fatal flaws characterize most research to date. First, studies cover too short a time span. Second, quality or type of software is not well controlled. Third, outcome measures—usually standardized tests—tap only a limited span of skills, and we need broader measures. . . . In short, the research on software's effectiveness is still limited, vague, and open to questions. Some computer use appears effective within a narrow set of educational objectives.

A respected large-scale national study by the Educational Testing Service on the impact of computers on learning mathematics found that when used selectively and by well-trained teachers, computers can significantly enhance academic performance for some students, particularly in upper grades. The 1998 report, which was sponsored by *Education Week* and the Milken Exchange, showed that eighth graders using computers to do complex mathematics problems such as simulations gained more than a third of an academic year in proficiency. However, for fourth graders who used computers for math games the benefits were negligible. The report concludes: "There may not be much opportunity to benefit from using computers before middle school." The findings underscore the importance of teacher training to help students derive the benefits of technology.

The question of computer use in schools, ultimately, is one of "how," not "whether." Finding the most effective methods and means is a major challenge facing both educational researchers and practitioners in the next decade.

Of course no technology or technique can supplant the efforts of trained education professionals, especially professionals who have access to and facility with the most effective educational technology. But it is also true that teachers—like their students, like all of society—will become increasingly reliant on that technology to learn and teach and communicate. In this sense, we are all guinea pigs in an experiment of our own making.

How One Multicultural School Makes Learning Cool

After wending their way through streets dominated by gangs, the students of the K-6 Juarez-Lincoln Accelerated School in south San Diego find a high-tech haven in the classroom. What began as a casual collaborative venture with a school 3,000 miles away has become a potent catalyst for systemic change at this classic "have-not" inner-city school, says principal Connie Smith. "We needed to do something to give our children the sense that learning is not only good but cool," she says.

While attending a conference in Chicago in 1993, Elizabeth Robinson, former assistant superintendent of the Chula Vista (CA) public school district, saw a presentation of Archaeotype, a computer-simulated archaeological dig developed by the elite Dalton School in New York City. The Dalton presenters—archaeologist Neil Goldberg, then-assistant headmaster Frank Moretti, and Luyen Cho, who at the time was director of the school's New Lab for Teaching and Learning—said they wanted to offer Archaeotype to a school without Dalton's considerable resources. Robinson approached them at the conference, and when she returned to California told Connie Smith about the exciting project from New York. Smith realized that this innovative technology might be just what she was looking for—a way to "provide stimulation for children in a working-class area with antisocial and gang elements."

In many respects, Juarez-Lincoln's student body is diverse—17 languages are represented, from Spanish and Vietnamese to Urdu. But in one significant way it is not: most of the students come from low-income homes. "Being poor is not a crime," says Smith, but since it does often translate into unequal access to technology, "providing the technology was our responsibility."

A three-year grant from Pacific Bell in 1995 made that possible. The money was given, in Smith's words, to "make a systemic change . . . change learning styles, add tools." The grant helped provide the teacher training and development as well as the technical support to implement Archaeotype and other programs. Smith describes Archaeotype as a "program in which children have to create and think and use those skills of discovery—higher-level skills—to make educated assumptions about ancient history." A further incentive for an educator ever mindful of standards: Archaeotype matched up nicely with California's sixth-grade social studies curriculum.

Getting the students interested in Archaeotype was easy. "The children jumped in without fear," Smith reports. "They are seduced by technology, which is a part of their lives." Working in groups, students examine "artifacts" of ancient Greece, Rome, and Persia, using the evidence to draw up hypotheses about life in those civilizations. For instance, a piece of jewelry might suggest something about the importance of appearance in certain segments of society. Students are required to cite three sources on which to base their conclusions. When new evidence surfaces or when classmates challenge their assumptions, the students must debate, revise, and refine their hypotheses. The process teaches them to be discriminating about resources and "not take at face value the first answer they receive" from the Internet or any other single source, says Smith.

"At the time, we could not even begin to think about matching Dalton's sophistication in terms of technology," Smith notes, but "we decided we could make it work." Using a 10-gigabyte server, four computers daisy-chained together, and a dot matrix printer, "the staff decided to make technology a tool for the youngsters to build on their strengths."

With the assistance of the Dalton School team, the students and teachers of Juarez-Lincoln set out on a new adventure. Jump-starting the project only a few months after the initial contact, Dalton brought Smith and three sixth-grade teachers—Bob Birdsell, Sharon Quinn, and Angela Shane—to New York to witness Archaeotype in action. Dalton also provided the Archaeotype disks, a 96-baud modem, a laser disk player, and copies of research materials. Goldberg also flew to San Diego for three short visits to work with the teachers and students.

Now the school has at least three computers in every classroom, including kindergarten. According to Smith, while only 5 percent of the students had access to computers at home in 1995, that percentage has escalated as parents have become more involved with their kids' adventures in computer technology. For instance, in one bilingual fourth-grade social studies class, parents help their children do research on Spanish missions as part of a section on California history. One student became intrigued by a piece of Peruvian glass he had virtually "unearthed." For the first time ever, he asked his mother to take him to the museum and the public library to do research. The student was so enthusiastic about what he learned that he produced his own report in addition to the group requirement.

The school also reaches out to neighborhood high school students. Since they may not have access to computers at home, they are allowed to use Juarez-Lincoln's facilities until about 6 P.M. to do research on the Internet. Those with afterschool jobs often call to make an appointment to access the web as late as 9 P.M. Elementary school students aren't the only ones discovering how cool learning can be.

For Further Information

Milken Exchange on Education Technology, 1250 Fourth St., Santa Monica, CA 90401-1353; tel: 310-998-2800; fax: 310-998-2828. www.mff.org

Educational Testing Service, Rosedale Rd., Princeton, NJ 08541; tel: 609-921-9000; fax: 609-734-5410; e-mail: etsinfo@ets.org. www.ets.org

Educational Technology Center, Harvard Graduate School of Education, Nichols House, Cambridge, MA 02138; tel: 617-495-9373; fax: 617-9268. http://gseweb.harvard.edu/~etc

The Media Lab, Massachusetts Institute of Technology, Bldg. E-15, 77 Massachusetts Ave., Cambridge, MA 02139-4307; tel: 617-253-0300; fax: 617-258-6264. www.media.mit.edu

Perseus Project, Classics Department, Tufts University, Eaton Hall, Medford, MA 02155; tel: 617-627-3213. www.perseus.tufts.edu

Archaeology's Dig, Archaeological Institute of America, 135 William St., New York, NY 10038; tel: 212-732-5154; fax: 212-732-5707. www.dig.archaeology.org

C. Norris, J. Smolka, and E. Soloway. "Convergent Analysis: A Method for Extracting the Value from Research Studies on Technology in Education." Paper presented at the

Secretary's Conference on Educational Technology, U.S. Department of Education, Washington, DC, July 1999. **www.ed.gov/Technology/TechConf/1999/whitepapers/ paper2.html**

J. Schacter. "The Impact of Education Technology on Student Achievement: What the Most Current Research Has to Say." Santa Monica, CA: Milken Exchange on Education Technology, June 1999. **www.mff.org/edtech/publication.taf?_function=detail&Content _uid1=161**

H. Wenglinsky. "Does it Compute? The Relationship between Educational Technology and Student Achievement in Mathematics." Princeton, NJ: Educational Testing Service, Policy Information Center, September 1998. **www.ets.org/research/pic/dic/preack.html**

J.M. Healy. *How Computers Affect Our Children's Minds—For Better and Worse.* New York: Simon & Schuster, 1998.

Commentary by George Brackett

"Technologies don't change schools— caring, capable people do"

Can new technologies, such as computers and the Internet, change schools in ways that other tools of reform have not? The Harvard Education Letter *asked George Brackett, director of the software development firm George Brackett Associates and a lecturer at Harvard's Technology in Education Program, to reply.*

Would we ask such a question about an *old* technology, one with which we're familiar, such as books or blackboards? "Can books change schools in ways that other tools of reform have not?"

That would be a silly question, of course. What kind of books? Written by whom? On what topics? Directed toward which learning goals? For which students? Used with what other educational resources? And with what pedagogical approach? We would want to know all of these things before venturing to say whether "books change schools." And we would never assume the answer to be independent of all the surrounding details.

Technologies do not change schools in any sense worth talking about. Thoughtful, caring, capable people change schools, sometimes with the help of technology, sometimes not, and sometimes even despite it. Too often we focus on the technology rather than the reform. Tell me the reform you want to enact, in some detail, and then I'll tell you which technologies might help.

Admittedly, some reforms might seem impossible without new technologies. How could elementary and middle school students participate actively in remote scientific expeditions without Internet-based linkages, for example? But the essential reform here is *not* the use of email and the web to connect the classroom to the field. It is the engagement of these students in doing real science, in collaboration with real scientists, instead of reading and talking about science and repeating memorized science factoids.

Internet technology facilitates and motivates the process. But without careful educational design and the guidance of a skilled teacher, such technologically enhanced experiences may not succeed at all. And the essence of the reform—engaging students in doing real science—has long been possible when accomplished with older technologies.

It's the pedagogy, not the technology, that's the key. New technologies are unreliable, expensive, and something new that both teachers and students have to learn to use. Only when a technology allows us to reach a hitherto inaccessible educational goal, or to reach an existing goal more effectively, should we consider employing it. It's a mistake to put technology center-stage as we plan and execute educational reforms. Technology should hover shyly in the wings, ready to lend its power, but only as needed.

Commentary by Edward Miller

"Technology is not just a tool"

Is technology just an educational tool or does it have more profound physical and psychological effects? We asked Edward Miller, a Cambridge, MA, education policy analyst and writer, and a former editor of the Harvard Education Letter, *to respond.*

One of the most common fallacies in discussions of technology and schooling is the argument that "the technology is just a tool." Computers, according to some advocates, are really no different from blackboards, overhead projectors, or textbooks; what's important is how we use them.

This argument is false first because our tools shape us and our ways of thinking about the world just as surely as we use them to reshape the world. Indeed, the development of the human brain over millions of years has been inextricably linked to the ways in which humans use tools. In his book *The Hand*, neurologist Frank R. Wilson describes how this works: changes in the structure of the human hand and arm, related to the need to grasp, throw, and manipulate objects like stones and sticks, led to changes in the structure of the brain and nervous system and the development of new, more complex patterns of thinking. This same process of co-evolution takes place in the development of individuals: children who learn to play the violin or piano, for example, develop neural networks that affect their ways of learning throughout life.

The "just a tool" argument is false in a second way: computer technology is fundamentally different from other kinds of tools used in education. It is, for some children, highly addictive in ways we are only beginning to document; and these technologies are being sold to schools and the public by an immensely rich and powerful corporate machine that bombards us daily with messages about their supposed benefits. America seems to be mesmerized by the amounts of money being made in the high-tech business and treats this success as proof that technology is always good. Meanwhile, the voices of caution and skepticism about technology's effects on children are invariably ridiculed as "Luddites" and, very often, silenced.

Technology is, most certainly, an enormously powerful tool that is reshaping teaching and learning in some highly questionable ways—especially in those schools that have rushed into its wholesale adoption. The greatest potential dangers are in the use of computers by young children, and the evidence of damage to their developing brains, bodies, and social selves will in all likelihood not become obvious for years, perhaps decades. It is for this reason, among others, that Frank Wilson argues that computers should be banned entirely from elementary education. I agree with him.

Can Technology Exploit Our Many Ways of Knowing?

By Howard Gardner

As human beings, we are the kinds of creatures who can learn in many ways: through exploration with our hands, the use of our several senses, the silent observations of other persons, conversation and argument, and the development of many different kinds of symbols—ranging from paintings or graphs to semaphore or dance notation. These alternative ways of knowing can often be observed at home, on the street, and, increasingly, in children's museums and other "hands-on" learning environments.

Regrettably, however, formal schooling often neglects these multiple ways of knowing. For the most part, youngsters sit in their seats all day, reading books or attending to lectures. When asked to show what they have learned, students typically take a written test—all too often, multiple choice—or are asked to recite back what they have read or heard.

It might seem that such "uniform schooling" is fair—since everyone is being treated in the same way. I believe, however, that it is fundamentally unfair. School has long privileged one or two forms of human intelligence—those involving language and logic—while ignoring the other powerful ways in which we can come to know the world.

According to Multiple Intelligences (MI) theory, all human beings possess at least eight forms of intelligence, which I call linguistic, logical-mathematical (the two favored in school), musical, spatial, bodily-kinesthetic, naturalist, interpersonal, and intrapersonal. All of us have these intelligences—they are what make us human, cognitively speaking. But because of genetic variation and the accidents of experience, no two of us have exactly the same blend or combination of intelligences. I call on educators to take advantage of this multiplicity of intelligences. Teachers should fashion teaching and learning so that *all* students have the chance to learn and to demonstrate what they have learned—not just those students who happen to be gifted with words and numbers.

The theory of multiple intelligences emerged during the same era as the "new technologies": CD-ROMs, videodisks, the Internet, the World Wide Web, and such promising approaches as lego-logo (where one can build elaborate physical structures by issuing commands at the keyboard) or hypermedia (where one can shift at will among written, graphic, and auditory contents and also rearrange those contents as one likes). It has seemed evident to many people—teachers, parents, youngsters, entrepreneurs, technologists—that these technologies ought to be mobilized for better instruction. Indeed, the process of using technology to mobilize the multiple intelligences of students has already begun. Technologies and technologically based exhibitions in museums invite students to use several intelligences; moreover, even when one is simply typing on one's keyboard, one can "think" in spatial, musical, linguistic, or bodily intelligences.

But before declaring victory, it's important to record a few cautionary notes. First of all, even in my lifetime, many technologies—from slide projectors to television—have been touted as "the solution" to American education. Yet these technologies have had remarkably little impact on mainstream education. When plugged in, they are all too often simply used to "deliver" the same old "drill-and-kill" content.

Second, once a multiple intelligences perspective has been introduced, there is a reflexive impulse to test youngsters to see which intelligences they have or lack. This could be done with old-fashioned materials (e.g., musical instruments, abacuses) or online: in fact, hardly a week goes by without some new start-up suggesting that it is developing ways of measuring or nurturing the intelligences. While this impulse is not malevolent, it need not yield positive educational outcomes. We are hardly better off if we have eight labels (good in language, poor in spatial thinking, etc.) for children rather than two (smart or not). Nor does it mean much educationally simply to develop one or more intelligences for their own sake.

What Are Our Goals?

Technology is neither good nor bad in itself, nor can it dictate educational goals. A pencil can be used to write Shakespearean sonnets or to copy someone else's homework. The Internet can be used to engender enlightenment or hatred. Before embracing any new technology, we need to declare our educational goals and demonstrate how a particular technology can help us to achieve them. And of course we must provide adequate technical assistance if the technology is to be deployed effectively.

I favor two broad classes of educational goals. First, we should help students to become certain kinds of adults. If, for example, we want students to be civil to one another, we need to develop their interpersonal skills. This could be done by recording tense interactions on video and having students choose the best human(e) means of reducing the tension; by involving students in chat-rooms or discussion forums that include opportunities for helpfulness or deceit; or by creating cartoon simulations or virtual reality scenarios of human dilemmas where the student has options to interact in various ways. Or, if we want students to be sensitive to the arts, we should let them examine different works of art and encourage them to create in words, musical sequences, or line, color, and form. While such opportunities have always existed, technology brings them literally to our fingertips: for example, one can compose (or at least "assemble") music at a computer even if one can neither read music nor play an instrument.

Second, we should help students to understand the major ways of thinking that have developed in the disciplines. Here is where the new technologies can really come into their own. In science, students need to understand how one develops theories, evaluates data, tests hypotheses, and makes predictions. Suppose, for example, one is learning to predict weather, or identify the strata of rocks in a region. With new software and the World Wide Web, it is possible to receive and to manipulate all kinds of (hopefully accurate) data, captured in a wide range of symbol systems, and evaluate respective claims and counterclaims.

Turning to the case of history, students need to understand how one makes sense of original documents, conflicting testimony, the oral, written, and graphic records in order to reconstruct events from the past. Again, suppose one is studying the causes of the First World War or the strategic battles of the Civil War. Using videodisks or CD-ROMs, one can easily access the relevant documents, including photographs or film records, create one's own models, evaluate them in the light of contemporary and retrospective accounts, and relate them to events in today's newspaper.

Don't get me wrong. Such scientific and historical studies could have been carried on in an earlier era, without benefit of multimedia or cybercommunication. But the new technologies make the materials vivid, easy to access, and fun to play with—and they readily address the multiple ways of knowing that humans possess. Moreover, for the first time ever, it is possible for teachers and other experts to examine the work efficiently, at long distances, and to provide quick and relevant feedback in forms that are useful to students.

Clearly, a marriage of education and technology could be consummated. But it will only be a happy marriage if those charged with education remain clear on what they want to achieve for our children and vigilant that the technology serves these ends. Otherwise, like other technologies, the new ones could end up spawning apathy, alienation, or yet another phalanx of consumers.

Copyright © 2000 by Howard Gardner

New Independence for Special Needs Students

From voice recognition to virtual reality, new technologies are helping classrooms and curricula become more inclusive

By Karen Kelly

Twelve-year-old Andrew Ashe has always loved stories. He spins tales of family camping trips and composes action-packed superhero stories in which he takes on the villains. But until recently, it was almost impossible for Andrew to put his stories down on paper. He has a familial tremor in his hands—so pronounced that he can barely hold a pencil. And he's dyslexic, which means that the words he does get on paper are often spelled wrong beyond recognition. "Before, it would take me so long just to write a sentence," says Andrew, who lives in Cambridge, MA. "I was always a great story writer, but I just couldn't get it down."

Andrew tried using a keyboard. His tremor caused him to hit the same key over and over, sending the letter across the page. Meanwhile, homework assignments piled up, and Andrew became increasingly discouraged. Then someone suggested he try voice-recognition software that translates speech into written text.

"He flies through his assignments now. His composing and reading skills have improved dramatically," says Tom Ashe, Andrew's father. "He wrote his first three-page story this summer, and when he told the computer to print, he was grinning from ear-to-ear."

At one time, students like Andrew didn't have many options. Most were relegated to special education classes, where their physical and learning disabilities blocked their access to learning, and their potential was cut short. Assistive technology has changed all that. Today, students who have never spoken can borrow a voice from their computers. Children who have trouble using their hands are writing with the help of specially designed computer mice and software programs that can predict the word they're trying to type. And researchers are experimenting with virtual reality programs that teach autistic children how to navigate busy streets safely.

As these new technologies help bridge the gap between childhood disabilities and learning, they also promise to make classrooms and curricula more inclusive. The distinctions between "special needs kids" and "kids who need some help" probably won't be as stark in the near future.

"The technology has changed dramatically," says Carol Cunningham, an educator in the Communication Enhancement Center (CEC) at Children's Hospital in Boston. "When I started working with assistive technology in the late 1980s, you could know everything that was out there; there was a set amount of things. Now, it's like knowing everything in the Boston Public Library."

New software and products arrive almost daily in Cunningham's small office. There's a pile of keyboards—some have enlarged keys that are easier to see and push, others come with pictures of objects such as apples and bears that allow disabled students to communicate an entire word with one keystroke.

Cunningham tries out each of these products and then matches the right technology to the disabled students who come to the CEC for consultation. "These tools give disabled kids greater independence. They're able to speak out loud, interact with other people, even play for the first time," she says, sifting through a blue Tupperware container filled with a collection of joysticks, roller balls, and traditional computer mice. "The first time a nonverbal child writes a sentence on the computer and then hears it spoken out loud, it's thrilling. They want to stay and keep writing."

An Extra Set of Hands

One of technology's biggest obstacles for physically disabled students is the computer keyboard. Kids with severe physical limitations such as cerebral palsy lack the muscle control to manipulate small keys. It's a disability that astrophysicist Stephen Hawking shares. He also may be the best-known user of "single-switch" technology, which enables him to communicate through a computer by pushing a button near his hand without speaking or typing. Many special educators say the single switch has changed the lives of severely disabled students more than any other technology. Cunningham says she was amazed at the "switching speed" used by Hawking during a recent visit to CEC.

"We can attach a switch to any part of the body—an eyelash, a cheek. We even had one person with a dental plate they could activate with their tongue," says Patti Slobogin, director of the Hudson Valley Regional Technology Center (HVRTC), a state-funded assistive technology institute in Valhalla, NY. "For someone physically locked in, it's amazing. It gives them access to the world."

The distinctions between "special needs kids" and "kids who need some help" probably won't be as stark in the near future.

These switches allow the user to scan a computer screen. The screen displays information such as numbers and letters. One at a time, large sections are highlighted. The user activates the switch when the section of the screen they want is highlighted. The program then becomes more specific, highlighting one line and then one letter at a time. With each movement, the user gets closer to choosing the letter or number they want. Slowly, this activity builds words and sentences at the bottom of the page, which the computer can read out loud.

"We saw one 19-year-old who had no voice and whose arms had atrophied. Nobody had any sense of what was going on inside of him," says Slobogin. "We found out he could move his head and provided him with a switch, attached to his chair, which he could press with a turn of his head. He picked it up very quickly. He even participated in his own [educational] evaluation and talked about it. Everyone was in tears."

While switches continue to be the most commonly used tool in alternative communication, the technology is advancing rapidly. One of the newest innovations used by disabled students is called the "head mouse." This shiny silver sticker with the circumference of a pencil eraser attaches to a student's forehead. When he moves his head, the cursor moves. A small box on the computer screen tracks the sticker's reflection and instructs the cursor to move accordingly. By using a head mouse instead of a single switch, the student doesn't have to wait for the screen to scan—he can make his choices instantly.

A similar invention uses infrared lasers to track where the user's eyes are focusing. The device then moves the cursor to the spot where the student's gaze is fixed.

Another way software developers have skirted the cumbersome pace of single switching is through the creation of word prediction—a computer program that has once again changed the way people with disabilities communicate.

Whether students use switches or keyboards, a box appears on the screen as soon as they enter the first letter, giving them a choice of commonly used words beginning with that letter. The choices change with each new letter. Once students spot the word they want, they can choose that number and the entire word appears. Word prediction significantly reduces the amount of typing or "switching" a disabled student needs to do.

"For people with physical disabilities, word prediction can save them an enormous amount of time," says Chuck Hitchcock, the lab director at the not-for-profit Center for Applied Special Technology (CAST) in Peabody, MA. "It's an important development in the way people who use switches communicate."

Speaking for the First Time

Once severely disabled children begin communicating through the computer, their lives change. For the first time, children with severe disabilities caused by illnesses such as cerebral palsy, Lou Gehrig's disease, and muscular dystrophy can have conversations with parents, teachers, and friends. But communication on a computer screen has its limits. If someone walks out of the room, the conversation stops because that person can no longer read the text on the screen. That's a situation where synthesized speech, or voice output, can make a difference.

"It's a feeling of empowerment," explains Shannon Elliott, a speech language pathologist at Children's Hospital in Boston. "When disabled children use it, people actually stop, turn around, and look at them. They can communicate over a greater distance."

When using synthesized speech, the child enters letters into the computer and the program reads along. Then the computer says each word and, after a period is typed, the sentence. This "talking" software gives children choices of male or female voices. One program even offers a voice called "cellos," which reads every word on the screen as if it's a Gregorian chant. Some educators have found the melodic tone can prompt nonspeaking children with autism to start singing along.

Synthesized speech programs read not only what the student enters but also any other text on the page. As a result, they can also provide support for the visually impaired and learning-disabled students who struggle with reading and writing. "Synthesized speech can really help a learning-disabled student because if the child types in a word and hears the computer pronounce something different, they know it needs to be corrected," says Patti Slobogin of HVRTC.

Synthesized speech programs may be the most effective way for students with learning disabilities to correct errors in their writing, according to researcher Marshall Raskind of the Frostig Center in Pasadena, CA. In one study, Raskind had 33 college students listen to another person read their text aloud and then listen to the computer read it out loud. The students detected the largest number of errors when the computer read their work back to them. "When you proofread yourself, there's a tendency to [inadvertently] fill in the gaps. But the computer actually tells it like it is," says Raskind. "And in the case of using another person to read it out loud, the student may be distracted by the presence of that other person. It's different when it's just them and the computer."

Synthesized speech programs can also be used for students who are simply poor readers and may find class content too difficult to read. Hearing textbooks read out loud can challenge and improve the student's skills and comprehension. CAST's eReader software uses synthesized speech and synchronized highlighting to help students with reading. eReader exemplifies CAST's "universal design" philosophy, which is that software and learning models should be usable not just by certain groups of students but by children with all kinds of physical and learning disabilities—or, just as important, by those with none at all.

Chuck Hitchcock of CAST says the teacher needs to decide when the synthesized speech program is appropriate, and when it's not. "If a student's reading skills are being tested, the synthesized speech function should be turned off," says Hitchcock. "But if they're learning social studies and it will take them hours to read what the other kids learn in 20 minutes, that's the time to use it. They need to have access to the general curriculum."

However, Raskind has found it may benefit some disabled students more than others. "The greater the disability, the more it helped. The lesser the disability, the more it interfered with comprehension," says Raskind. He found the computer's auditory feedback could be distracting, causing the student to lose track of a selection's context. "For those kids who are trying to read and listen at the same time, it can be a cognitive overload."

When This User Talks, the Computer Listens

Like Cambridge student Andrew Ashe, 17-year-old Geralyn Miller can barely grasp a pencil. But in her case, the obstacle is pain. Miller has fibromyalgia, a chronic illness that causes painful spasms in her neck and shoulders. Whenever she tries to write or type an assignment, the pain gets worse. So Miller decided to try using a speech recognition system that converts her speech into text on the page.

"It's definitely more pain-free. Before, I kind of dreaded writing assignments," says Miller, a student at Barnstable High School in Hyannis, MA. "Now, I can get my homework done on time. And my teachers say my writing has improved."

For bright, motivated students like Geralyn Miller, speech recognition software can offer a significant bridge over a disability that has prevented them from fully participating in school. But Bob Follansbee, co-director of the Speak to Write project at Boston's Education Development Center, says the technology has its drawbacks.

"First, you have to spend a good ten hours training the software to recognize your voice. Then, you have to learn how to run the word processing functions at the same time you're dictating your text. And, most important, you have to learn how to compose using speech," says Follansbee, who conducts training sessions and hosts a "listserv" for speech recognition users in schools. "The process by which you think is very different. You must be aware of what you want to say, have it more or less composed in your head before you speak it, and you have to supply all the punctuation by voice."

In the case of younger children, Follansbee says it's imperative that an adult is trained in the software as well. Andrew Ashe's mother, Kathy, was her son's primary trainer. She attended a week-long seminar last summer along with Andrew's teacher. She says it requires hard work and discipline on the part of the adult and the child.

"When you first start, almost every word you say will be wrong. So you have to make corrections until the computer gets used to your voice," says Ashe. "It's not easy to sit there for 15 hours in the summer with someone who would rather be out swimming."

Parental and teacher support is crucial in the use of any assistive technology. But speech recognition may offer the best example of what can happen when adults fail to get involved. On the one hand, Andrew Ashe's experience with speech recognition encouraged other teachers in the Cambridge school district to learn the system. But when it was introduced to a child born with no hands, his teacher and parents failed to get involved. They didn't pursue training and were unable to help him incorporate it into his schoolwork or his life at home. As a result, he was never able to use it. "If a couple of people drop the ball, it just doesn't happen," says Follansbee. "I always feel terrible, but I think the situation is improving."

For those students who do persevere, the research suggests their academic skills improve as well. Marshall Raskind studied learning-disabled students who were struggling to get their thoughts down on paper. Nineteen students used speech recognition for 50 minutes a week, while a control group of 20 students did not. The speech recognition group showed significantly more improvement than the control group in word recognition, spelling, and reading comprehension.

"They get simultaneous auditory and visual input because they're monitoring the words on the screen as they speak. If there's an error, they have to choose the correct word from a box of choices," says Raskind. "So it's not only a tool to overcome their disability, it also improves reading and writing skills."

Deaf students can benefit from speech recognition as well. In mainstream classrooms, an interpreter sitting next to a deaf student can listen to the teacher and repeat the words into the computer, while the deaf student reads the output. Carl Jensema, vice president of the Institute for Disabilities Research and Training in Silver Spring, MD, says this has great potential in the deaf community: "Speech recognition technology is the Holy Grail of deaf people. I am confident that someday, within my lifetime, speech recognition technology will be good enough to replace a sign language interpreter in all but the most demanding interpreting situations."

Looking into the Future

Peggy Roblyer and Bill Wiencke believe they're working on the next great development in assistive technology—virtual reality. The State University of West Georgia researchers say they can see the day when children confined to wheelchairs will experience the sensation of running and jumping. They also point to autistic and developmentally delayed students as potential beneficiaries.

Finding financial backing will be a challenge, however, because so few potential investors believe virtual reality is feasible, they say. "It's so difficult for people to see the utility of virtual reality for special needs students; it's hard to show them the possibilities," says Roblyer. "There's so much potential that hasn't been explored."

In fact, experiments have shown these dreams can become a reality. In one, physically disabled children donned virtual reality headgear and used a mouse to navigate a program that created the illusion that they were swimming. Their job was to catch sharks in a big net. The game prompted them to try new movements with their body, and it allowed them, through a realistic-looking three-dimensional program, to simulate the experience of swimming. Wiencke says the purpose of this program is mainly to stimulate kids, to get them moving and playing. While some may question whether this would upset them by reminding them of the limits of their disability, Wiencke hasn't found that to be a problem.

"Kids don't seem to have all of that emotional baggage that adults have," says Wiencke. "They just say, 'Gee, that sounds neat,' whereas older people visualize it differently."

In Britain, where the bulk of research is being conducted, Middlesex University professor Nigel Foreman was interested in whether students would transfer the lessons they learned in virtual reality to real-world situations. He found disabled children who learned to navigate a school building with virtual reality were able to apply that knowledge when they were placed in the actual school. Similar results were found with two autistic children who were taught how to safely cross the street. In fact, the researchers found the virtual-reality training also improved the students' ability to navigate in other settings.

At Israel's Bar-Ilan University, David Passig has used virtual-reality training with deaf students. Previous researchers have found that students who are hard of hearing have a difficult time using inductive reasoning—drawing on specific examples of something to make a broader generalization. For instance, they may have trouble identifying what apples, oranges, and bananas have in common.

In his study, Passig asked a group of deaf children to play the computer game Tetris, in which the player moves the pieces on the screen into empty spaces of the same shape. Half of the students played a two-dimensional version of the game and the other half played the game in 3-D, or virtual reality. Passig found that the students who used the 3-D version showed improvement in their ability to use inductive thinking. In fact, their scores matched those of a control group of hearing children who had no intervention.

Until recently, virtual-reality programs were prohibitively expensive. The head-mounted displays alone cost thousands of dollars. But new software that can be used on a typical computer monitor may make virtual reality much more accessible. Peggy Roblyer cautions that many questions still need to be answered. "Now is the time to be exploring this. We can't go anywhere unless we experiment with these things," says Roblyer. "We don't know if the skills will transfer to the real world. We don't know if there will be side effects such as a false sense of safety. We still don't know any of these things."

As with any assistive technology, Roblyer knows that breakthroughs only happen when people are willing to dream. "You have to be a little bit of a visionary," says Roblyer. "You have to look at what there is today and see the possibilities for the future."

"We Realized the Curriculum Itself Was Broken"

When David Rose first met Matthew 15 years ago, Rose could tell the youngster was bright even though Matthew couldn't walk, talk, or move his hands. Educators had searched for ways to help Matthew adapt to the classroom, but his potential remained untapped. Rose, a lecturer in education at Harvard, decided to try a different approach. He and his colleagues created an electronic book that Matthew could manipulate using an infrared beam that tracked the movement of his eyes.

For the first time, Matthew could turn pages and "read" a book out loud. "Matthew forced us to change," says Rose. "Everything was designed with the thought that all students are the same. If not, people thought they needed some expensive stuff to fix them. What we realized was that the curriculum itself was broken, that we needed to start designing learning environments that were inclusive from the start."

That was 15 years and 83 electronic books ago. Today, Rose is co-director of the Center for Applied Special Technology (CAST), a not-for-profit organization in Peabody, MA, dedicated to "the creation of computer software and learning models that are usable by everyone." Educational computer software, says Rose, doesn't have to support just one disability, such as blindness, but can be used by children with all kinds of physical and learning disabilities—or by those with none at all.

Rose calls this concept "universal design." For instance, once a textbook is on CD-ROM, children who are blind or have difficulty reading can ask the computer to read the text aloud. Kids who can't hold a book can turn pages on the computer with a click of the mouse. By not employing the program's special qualities, non-disabled kids can easily use the programs too. "It's the opposite approach of assistive technology. Rather than retrofitting existing programs, we create software that modifies itself to the kid," says Rose, who co-founded CAST in 1984 with Anne Meyer, a clinical psychologist with a doctorate in education from Harvard.

For instance, there's the eReader, a talking browser that supports students with reading and sight disabilities. The software places an additional toolbar on the top of the screen that can be used with any computer text, including web pages. As it reads the text out loud, the words are highlighted simultaneously. "This lets [disabled] students work side by side with kids who don't have these disabilities," says Chuck Hitchcock, the director of CAST's Universal Design Lab. "In classes like social studies, we need them to be able to learn the content of the curriculum without worrying about the struggle of reading."

In fact, schools are now legally obligated to include disabled students in every aspect of the curriculum. When the Individuals with

Disabilities Education Act (IDEA) was amended in 1997, lawmakers added the requirement that disabled students had to be exposed to the same curriculum and assessments as everyone else. They also required that the schools provide whatever technological tools these students needed for access.

A Budget-Friendly Idea

David Rose says this came as a shock to many educators. "The reaction was, 'Oh my God, the autistic kids are supposed to learn U.S. history?'" says Rose. "For the first time, schools are being held accountable for what these kids are learning." As administrators have begun to recognize the enormity of that task, Rose has found the idea of universal design—of providing educational material that every student can use—is catching on. "Schools have limited budgets. They can't spend $40,000 on one kid," says Rose. "So, they're starting to look for a curriculum that's accessible to everybody."

The U.S. Department of Education has embraced the concept as well. CAST was recently given a five-year grant to create the National Center on Accessing the General Curriculum. Patty Guard, acting director of the department's Office of Special Education Programs, says the center's mission is to help implement the changes made in IDEA. "We need to make sure that the government and district policies that are developed are in alignment with the goals of the law," says Guard. "We also need to ensure that research is being done and that the findings of that research make it into the classroom."

So, while schools scramble to implement programs giving disabled children access to the general curriculum, researchers are being called on to test the effectiveness of these programs. In that sense, CAST may have an advantage in the field, since it is led by educational experts with proficiency in technology—rather than technology buffs with an interest in education.

CAST has joined with other organizations to help meet the requirements of the grant and will take the lead in creating universally designed curricula. Another partner, the Council for Exceptional

Children, will make sure disabled children are represented. Meanwhile, Boston College's teacher education program will lead the professional development component. And faculty at Harvard Law School will help ensure that policies reflect the changes in IDEA.

One of the biggest challenges lies in persuading textbook publishers to get involved. David Rose hopes to create a digital library, which will carry CD-ROM versions of common textbooks that schools can purchase for their disabled students. Rose would prefer that CD-ROM versions were distributed automatically with every textbook, but he has found publishers reluctant to do that. "The publishers fear the CD-ROMs will be distributed as free copies of the textbook. They want to be fairly compensated," says Rose. "Part of our job will be to set standards to ensure that [compensation] happens."

One of the first publishers to agree to a CD-ROM version is Houghton Mifflin. This year it distributed social studies textbooks for the first through eighth grades on CD-ROM. However, the company's media projects manager, Nancy Dasho, is quick to point out that multimedia is not meant to replace traditional textbooks.

"This is for some children but not for all," says Dasho. "We advocate that disabled students use this in conjunction with the textbook. That way, if they're reading at the same time as other students, they won't look different."

But the idea of distributing books to some children and CD-ROMs to others doesn't fit the definition of universal design. Rose hopes to eliminate some of the publishers' reluctance by using the National Center on Accessing the General Curriculum as a mediator between publishers concerned about losing profits and schools that need universally accessible textbooks.

Patty Guard believes CAST's concept of universal design is a near-perfect solution for bringing schools into compliance with the new IDEA regulations. "It makes so much more sense than customizing just any curriculum that's been designed," says Guard. "This will cast the net broadly—relying on computer software that's usable by everybody. Students with disabilities will finally be learning what everyone else is."

For Further Information

Center for Applied Special Technology, 39 Cross St., Peabody, MA 01960; tel: 978-531-8555; e-mail: cast@cast.org. www.cast.org

Communication Enhancement Center, Children's Hospital, 300 Longwood Ave., Boston, MA 02115; tel: 617-355-6460. www.childrenshospital.org

Bob Follansbee, Speak to Write Project, Education Development Center, 55 Chapel St., Newton, MA 02458; tel: 617-969-7100; e-mail: BFollansbee@edc.org. www.edc.org/spk2wrt

LD OnLine: The Interactive Guide to Learning Disabilities. An interesting web site offering bulletin boards, "Ask the Expert," and a free newsletter. www.ldonline.org

D. Passig. "Virtual Literacy: Literacy in Virtual Learning Environments." In H.F. Didsbury, ed., *Future Vision: Ideas, Insights and Strategies,*.Washington, DC: World Future Society, 1996.

Marshall Raskind, Frostig Center, 971 N. Altadena Dr., Pasadena, CA 91107; e-mail: center@frostig.org.

M.H. Raskind, E.L. Higgins, N.B. Slaff, and T.K Shaw. "Assistive Technology in the Homes of Children with Learning Disabilities: An Exploratory Study." *Learning Disabilities: A Multidisciplinary Journal* 9, no. 2 (Summer 1998): 47–56.

M.H. Raskind, R.J. Goldberg, E.L. Higgins, and K.L. Herman. "Patterns of Change and Predictors of Success in Individuals with Learning Disabilities: Results from a Twenty-Year Longitudinal Study. *Learning Disabilities Research & Practice* 14, no. 1 (Winter 1999): 35–49.

M.D. Roblyer and J. Edwards. *Integrating Educational Technology into Teaching* (2nd ed.). Saddle River, NJ: Prentice-Hall, 1999.

Margaret Roblyer, State University of West Georgia, College of Education, Carrollton, GA, 30118; e-mail: mrobyler@westga.edu.

D. Rose and A. Meyer. *Learning to Read in the Computer Age.* Cambridge, MA: Brookline Books, 1998.

Patti Slobogin, Director, Lower Hudson Valley Regional Technology Center, Westchester Institute for Human Development, Cedarwood Hall, Valhalla, NY 10595; e-mail: patti_slobogin@nymc.edu.

T. Woronov. "Assistive Technology for Literacy Produces Impressive Results for the Disabled." *Harvard Education Letter* 10, no. 5 (September/October 1994): 6–7.

Commentary by Thomas Hehir

"Some assessments treat learning-disabled students unfairly"

If special needs students can take advantage of new technologies to improve their learning, why can't they use those same technologies to demonstrate what they've learned via high-stakes tests? HEL asked Thomas Hehir, a lecturer at the Harvard Graduate School of Education and a distinguished scholar at the Education Development Center in Newton, MA, to reply.

A recent *Boston Globe* article profiled a young man with impaired vision who had failed the high school English test because the state guidelines would not allow him to use his computer or other accommodations he needed to perform the test. This article highlighted an important issue in standards-based reform: in the assessment process, many students with disabilities are being denied the use of technologies that have enabled them to gain access to the curriculum and learn the skills and content being tested. In states where high-stakes decisions are based on these assessments, students may very well be denied promotion or graduation unfairly.

New technologies have greatly expanded educational opportunity for students with disabilities. Students who cannot speak through their own voice box can do so through talking computers. Blind students can take notes in class with braille-and-voice devices. Those with learning disabilities can produce term papers with the help of word processing and modified spell checks. These technologies, and many more, expand the ability of disabled students to access the same curriculum taught to their nondisabled peers. As one disability advocate testified in a hearing for the National Institute for Disability and Rehabilitation Research, "Technology improves life for nondisabled people. Technology makes life possible for many disabled people." This is certainly true for many students in our schools who have disabilities.

Though all states allow for some adjustments in the administration of their statewide assessments, anecdotal evidence would suggest that some states are not allowing for the full range of accommodation needed by students with disabilities. For instance, a state might offer the print disabled, such as those with visual impairments or dyslexia, an untimed test for an assessment in English, but not allow them to use taped texts. Or spell checks may be denied to learning-disabled students in writing assessments even though accurate spelling may be nearly impossible for that child.

By not allowing disabled students the use of the full range of technologies and accommodations in the administration of state and local assessments, we are effectively requiring them to be nondisabled when testing time rolls around. This is unfair and potentially illegal.

The simple solution is to allow these students the same assistance in the assessment process as they have in the learning process. Students with disabilities have demonstrated that there is not one way to walk, speak, read, or write. New educational technologies have made this possible. Therefore, it is only fair that the assessment of what they have learned should allow for them to demonstrate their knowledge and skills in the way most appropriate to them.

Distance Learning in the Digital Age

"E-courses" are much more than digital-age adaptations of the old correspondence courses

By Natalie Engler

In a corner of Hudson (MA) High School's computer lab, senior Amanda Ponte goes online and finds the assignment sheet for a netcourse called Perspectives in Health. She clicks the mouse on Week 8 and learns that she has to read chapters five through eight in *The Outsiders*, S.E. Hinton's 1967 novel about disaffected teens. She's also asked to write a short essay about the various cliques in her school. She's not quite sure what *The Outsiders* has to do with health, so she'll e-mail her teacher and find out.

Across the room, Ryan Neuffer clicks a mouse and the Beatles start to sing "When I'm 64." He's taking a course called Web Writing and learning how to write multimedia short stories that are enhanced by illustrations, videos, and music. He wrote a short story that opens: "It all started 48 years ago . . ." The Beatles song provides a clue. Ryan is 16 now—"That means I'd be 64 when I'm writing the story," he points out.

The class, says Ryan, teaches more than JavaScript and HTML. In addition to improving his writing skills, he is learning how to give and take constructive criticism and how to improve his work through revision. The extra hours spent tweaking web pages in the lab and at home at night has less to do with earning good grades than with achieving a sense of personal accomplishment, not to mention approval from his peers. Says Ryan: "When I make changes. I feel good. I think, 'People will like it now.'"

Across the country, hundreds of students are now participating in high school distance-learning courses. Amanda and Ryan take their cyberclasses through the Virtual High School (VHS), the pioneer online program launched in October 1996 by the Hudson (MA) Public Schools and The Concord Consortium's Educational Technology Lab in Concord, MA. VHS began with a $7.5 million five-year Technology Innovation Challenge Grant from the Department of Education. In its first three years, the number of high schools participating in VHS grew from 30 to 120, representing 26 states. In 1999–2000, 107 teachers taught 87 courses to approximately 1,800 students, while another 130 teachers are in VHS training. Participating schools and students cover a broad range—urban, rural farming, and suburban communities; college preparatory schools; two schools for the deaf; and six international schools in places like Singapore, Spain, and Venezuela.

In the next few years, these kinds of opportunities for distance learning are likely to increase dramatically as universities and for-profit companies follow VHS's lead, and the U.S. Department of Education (DOE) continues to give out seed money to such projects. States like Georgia, Massachusetts, and Ohio are exploring ways to enable all of their high schools to take part in VHS or other such distance-learning programs. Online courses are springing up in places like Kentucky, Florida, and Washington State. The North Dakota statewide public school system, the University of Texas at Austin, and Indiana University all offer high school classes online.

In 1999, the DOE gave $15 million in start-up money to Class.com, a Lincoln, NE, company that will market online high school courses developed by the University of Nebraska's Department of Distance Education. The venture is an extension of Nebraska's successful "snail-mail" correspondence course system, in which students received assignments and course materials through the postal service and returned their completed work to a teacher miles away the same way. Of course, the revolutionary technologies employed in online learning make such "e-courses" much more than a mere digital-age adaptation of the old correspondence courses.

A Pioneering Effort

In the Virtual High School—the best-known online distance learning program—each participating school offers at least one online class, or "netcourse," to the consortium. The netcourse is designed and conducted by one of the school's teachers, who gets training and support from VHS teaching mentors and technical experts. Teachers learn to moderate online discussions and create assignments that let students take advantage of the vast resources of the Internet. For every course a school contributes, it can sign up 20 of its students for other VHS courses. Each school also designates a site coordinator, who provides administrative and technical support for both teachers and students.

Students access their course site using a standard web browser (like Netscape) and a password. They can view, print, and respond to material posted on the course's web site by the teacher and other students. The courses are delivered through software called LearningSpace from IBM's Lotus division, which has donated software licenses and technical support as a VHS sponsor. LearningSpace has five interactive databases and tools, including a schedule, a profile of students and the teacher, a media center for assignments, a course room for threaded discussions so students can follow a conversation from the original question or topic through all related tangents, and an assessment area.

> **"It isn't for everyone . . . but distance learning gives kids experience in being independent and self-directed. It teaches them to use the Internet in a valuable way."**

Students typically take a netcourse during the day as one of their regular courses. Some schools, such as the Model School for the Deaf at Gallaudet University, designate a period for all VHS students to work together in the computer lab. Others let students use the computers in a lab or media center any time they have space available. Most follow a weekly rhythm that includes a major topic, assigned activities, online discussions, and student contributions. Except in rare circumstances, students are not allowed to fill their schedules with netcourses or to enroll in courses already offered by their schools.

One of the great advantages of online learning is that the Internet and e-mail make it possible to conduct courses quickly and efficiently. A small school participating in a distance-learning program like VHS may potentially offer as many courses to its students as a large school. For example, VHS offerings range from advanced academic courses like AP Statistics to technical and specialty elective courses such as Business in the 21st Century, Music Appreciation and Composition, and Cyber-Reporting.

Online learning also gives students access to expensive or hard-to-get resources. In a VHS course called Photography as Visual History, teacher Susan Leavey of Marlborough (MA) High School posts galleries of photos. "We were able to go see stuff they have in the New York City museums without having to leave our hometowns," says Melinda Miller-Klopfer, who took the netcourse last year from her home in Gualala, CA.

Proponents say netcourses teach students new technologies and on-line teamwork—essential skills for the 21st century—as they take part in online discussions, research on the Internet, and develop multimedia presentations either alone or in groups to demonstrate their understanding of subject matter. "It isn't for everyone and it isn't 'The Answer,' but it is a unique experience for these kids," says Leavey. "It gives them experience in being independent and self-directed. It teaches them to use the Internet in a valuable way."

Online learning may also eliminate some of the social stigmas that accompany so much of high school life. In a netcourse, nobody is overweight, has acne, or has a stutter. Students can't laugh at each other or interrupt while someone is collecting his thoughts.

Since much netcourse communication is asynchronous, meaning that the teacher and students are not necessarily online at the same time, "discussion" often has the potential to go beyond what is feasible in a 40-minute class period. Students and teachers may respond to previous comments, ask questions, post assignments, and give feedback at any time of day. Furthermore, unlike in regular conversation, web "conversations" give students instant transcripts: they can literally look back over previous discussions and weave together new ideas with those already expressed.

The fact that netcourse students come from varied regions and school systems can also strengthen discussions. "I find the level of discourse is much deeper than I've experienced in face-to-face classes," says Marsha West, an English teacher at Forks (WA) High School. In her VHS course on Greek drama, West says that a student from an urban arts high school who has experience staging an ancient Greek-style play may be able to lead an informative conversation on the subject. Meanwhile, a very shy student who knows a great deal about history, drama, and mythology may be more willing to communicate that knowledge in an online environment than she would in a normal classroom.

That freedom from time and place may make online classes an attractive option for schools that are looking for effective ways to reach students who may have difficulty attending regular classes—students with disabilities, for example. "Our deaf students can participate with hearing students without needing interpreters," says site coordinator Joyce Barrett of the Model Secondary School for the Deaf at Gallaudet University.

Challenges and Drawbacks

While netcourses may seem like a great enhancement to learning, virtual education is not without critics. Lowell Monke, an instructor at Grinnell College and co-author of the forthcoming book, *Breaking Down the Digital Walls*, has spent eight years designing and coordinating virtual-education projects with students. In his experience, "Any time we start doing telecommunication as a means of education, we enter an environment that is extremely diminished," he says, adding that it takes away body language, facial expression, tone of voice, and easily discernible sarcasm.

Contrary to West's experience, Monke has found it difficult to have a genuine dialogue between students who don't know each other. Students do not seem to trust one another, he says, and misunderstandings are easier in a faceless online environment. Moreover, he contends, teachers may become so enamored with the technology that they may ignore the valuable, offline resources right under their noses—local newspapers, say, or museums. "Every time you add a computer it's a substitution, not a supplement," says Monke.

Overall, the students who do best in netcourses are focused, self-directed, independent, motivated, and comfortable expressing themselves in writing. While many students thrive on the experience, others have dropped classes because they've fallen behind or because they needed face-to-face interaction with their teacher and peers.

VHS administrators say that for a netcourse to be successful, teachers need to encourage substantive interactions among students, monitor and shape the conversation, and promote an atmosphere where students respond to others' work. That may require a far greater commitment of time and energy than some students are used to giving, and those that underestimate the work it entails can spoil a course for their students.

What's Next?

VHS's first year, 1996–1997, was plagued by crashing servers, buggy software, and a faculty comprised largely of telecollaboration novices. Many of those wrinkles seem to have been ironed out. SRI International's Center for Technology in Learning, a Silicon Valley research institute, conducted semiannual surveys and longitudinal case studies over VHS's first four years. During that time "there was in increase in satisfaction among all the participant groups," reports Andrew Zucker, program manager for SRI. "Teachers have learned how to use the medium better. The site coordinators in the schools understand the Virtual High School better. Everything is falling into place."

That recent evaluation may prove particularly important for VHS's future. The project's original Department of Education Challenge Grant will run out in 2001. A private foundation will fund the program through one additional year. After that, participating schools will have to pay a membership fee, which Bruce Droste, director of the Concord Consortium, which co-founded VHS, estimates will be about $6,000. That's on top of what schools spend to upgrade their electronic capabilities to participate in the program. Schools taking part must have the latest browser software and are encouraged to install high-speed Internet access lines. In addition, since students and teachers need daily Internet access for at least a full period, schools may need to buy more computers. Some participants say that their schools have spent close to $15,000 to $25,000 on technology upgrades alone. That's before investing to train teachers and site coordinators.

The creators of VHS have thought about these issues, according to Droste. But they determined that if netcourses are to be valuable, the program can't use lowest common denominator technology (that is, listservs and bulletin boards). Without the multimedia software, the courses could potentially end up as dry, text-based, one-on-one communication between the teachers and individual students. Instead, everyone involved can bring in all the Internet has to offer, including databases, sound, images, and video.

"Some schools used this project as a lever with their school board to get the technology they needed. Others had the technology but didn't know what to do with it. But for schools that don't have it," Droste concedes, "there's no way they can get to us yet."

VHS has made some progress in finding a wider audience. SRI determined that during the first year of VHS, a majority of students came from relatively affluent backgrounds, had above-average or exceptional academic backgrounds, and were college bound, says Zucker. However, as early as the second year and beyond, VHS participants represented a broader range of students, a trend that is likely to continue as more core curriculum classes are offered, and as the digital divide in schools and homes shrinks.

To further broaden its scope, VHS will begin offering the Teachers Learning Conference to education students in university and college programs during the 2000–2001 school year. Those who complete the intensive course would continue to be supported by VHS as they enter their field placement and practicum.

Not that VHS is positioning itself as a substitute for traditional high schools. Quips Droste, "We don't want to take away the experience of kids bumping into each other at school."

What It Takes to Teach a Netcourse

Marsha West, a popular English teacher at Forks (WA) High School, was ready to give up teaching. "I was burned out," says the one-time Teacher of the Year who also chaired the English Department. After 20 years of teaching, she says, "I was tired of making people learn things they didn't want to learn."

But John Jones, the superintendent of schools in this small logging town on Washington's Olympic peninsula, had other ideas. He saw the potential of the Virtual High School program not only to offer Fork's 320 high school students more courses, but also to stimulate a star teacher such as West enough to convince her to stay on for a few more years.

He was right. West put off retirement to teach netcourses. She enjoys her virtual interactions with students from all over the country. And she thrives on the creative aspects of designing, refining, and teaching her netcourse.

Teaching a netcourse is very different from traditional teaching, says West, who teaches a 10th-grade honors netcourse called Web-Quest: A Literary Odyssey, which examines what it means to be a human being through the prism of classical mythology, philosophy, and drama. For a netcourse to be successful, she admits, teachers may need to work harder to encourage substantive interactions among students than they would in a traditional classroom. They have to monitor and shape online discussions, and encourage students to respond to one another's work. That usually requires a teacher to log on throughout the day to answer questions, monitor discussions, and give feedback. Otherwise, students can easily become confused, adrift, or apathetic.

So netcourse teachers need to be well organized and able to clearly articulate their instructions in writing. They don't have the luxury of reading students' faces to see who's confused. "It takes an immense amount of work to translate the kinds of things you do to make discussions successful in a classroom," says West. "You have to be facilitating all the time."

West goes online several times a day. She encourages students to post comments by typing in observations such as "Mary, look what they're doing over here" or "John, you haven't said anything in awhile. Let's get your thoughts on this topic." The software works well for collaborative work, she adds, "but it has to be made to happen by a teacher. It won't happen by itself."

VHS instructor Susan Leavey of Marlborough (MA) High School says the time ratio between a netcourse and a classroom-taught course is three or four to one. And that doesn't include the time spent in the Teacher Learning Conference, an intensive 125-hour graduate-level course teachers must complete before they're certified to teach in VHS. "In a single day, there could be 20 to 50 things I need to look at online and review," she says. "I spend almost all my free time at school at the computer."

In a netcourse, it's more important to be present than to be a performer, according to Bruce Droste. A teacher who is successful in the classroom may be less so online, and vice versa. "That teacher who is charismatic and who can walk into a classroom knowing the subject so well he can wing it—that teacher is not always good in this environment," says Droste. "We've taken away the classroom, the adoration, the electricity that might be going back and forth. We've de-egotized it."

An adventurous, risk-taking spirit doesn't hurt. Says Droste, "I've said to groups of teachers, 'Imagine being outside with four friends and you trip and fall into a mud puddle. If you're going to be embarrassed don't come to us. If you're going to dust yourself off and laugh and go on, come to us.'"

For Further Information

American Center for the Study of Distance Education, Penn State University, College of Education, 110 Rackley, University Park, PA 16802; tel: 814-863-3764; fax: 814-865-5878; e-mail: ACSDE@psu.edu. www.ed.psu.edu/ACSDE

Hudson Public Schools, 155 Apsley, Hudson, MA 01749; tel: 978-567-6100. www.hudson.k12.ma.us

Model Secondary School for the Deaf, Gallaudet University, 800 Florida Ave. NE, Washington, DC 20002; tel: 202-651-5340. http://clerccenter.gallaudet.edu/MSSD/index.html

L. Monke and R.W. Burniske. *Breaking Down the Digital Walls*. Albany: State University of New York Press, in press.

Virtual High School, Concord Consortium, 10 Concord Crossing, Concord, MA 01742; tel: 978-371-3484; fax: 978-371-3995; e-mail: vhsinfo@concord.org. http://vhs.concord.org/home.htm

SRI International's Center for Technology in Learning, 333 Ravenswood Ave., Menlo Park, CA 94025-3493. www.sri.com/policy/ctl/html/vhs.htm

The Global Schoolhouse

By connecting learners from Toronto to Kampala, the Web creates exciting opportunities and also new challenges, such as how to make sure global contacts are equitable and mutual

By Wambui Githiora-Updike

The three-week school vacation is over, and 15-year-old Wanjiku Thuku returns to her daily routine in Karen, a suburb of Kenya's capital city, Nairobi. Arriving home from school in early evening, she checks on her two young brothers, who got home earlier. They are fine. The temperature has dropped from nearly 80 degrees earlier in the day to a cool 60 degrees, and Wanjiku can see the shrubs and trees outside her family's spacious home sway in the winter evening breeze. She closes the windows. "Stay out, mosquitoes," she says to no one in particular. Afterward, she makes a cup of hot cocoa, then goes to the guest bedroom, turns on the computer, and signs on to Africaonline.

She has two e-mail messages waiting. One from her sister, Njeri, who has just returned to law school in the English midlands after a wonderful holiday in Kenya. "All is well," Njeri writes. "Tell everyone I'll write a longer one soon." The other message is from a school friend. They saw each other earlier in the day, of course, but when you're 15, there's always news to share that can't wait for tomorrow. She replies to both e-mails, then joins the rest of the family in the living room where her brothers are watching an American children's program.

Across town, at Arcade Cybercafe in the suburb of Westlands, all four computers are occupied by people who have signed on to the Internet to communicate with friends, join chat groups, or conduct research on a variety of topics. At the three public telephones, callers speak in various languages to friends and business associates in the city and abroad. An assistant is ready to help users reach their intended parties across town or cyberspace and, with the press of a key, quickly issues the necessary command to the computer or the telephone. With just a few keystrokes, this city in the highlands of East Africa is connected to

Oslo and London, Johannesburg and New Delhi—to wherever the Internet can be accessed.

The Internet has revolutionized communications, bringing about new relationships between ordinary people, business enterprises, government agencies, and all other consumers of ideas and products throughout the world. More than ever before, information itself has become a vital resource and commodity; the need to access it efficiently is felt throughout the world. For Wanjiku, a typical middle-class Kenyan teenager, logging on to the Internet has become as routine as turning on a radio or opening a book. Just as her parents started their cars without so much as thinking of Henry Ford, she considers global connectivity a given of everyday life.

As the 21st century unfolds, young Wanjiku and others like her will continue to share and consume information from all parts of the globe. Theirs is a generation with a new set of tools with which to negotiate the world. The rapid proliferation of Internet-accessible databases can be taken as evidence of this and as a harbinger of what's to come. As of September 1999, an estimated 216 million people were using the Internet every day, according to the World Bank. Of these, 1.8 million lived in Africa, 4 million in Latin America, 37.2 million in Asia, 53.5 million in Europe, 119 million in North America, and nearly 1 million in the Middle East. Africaonline was the brainchild of Kenyan graduates of MIT and other U.S. universities. It has become the leading provider of Internet services throughout Africa, with offices in major English- and French-speaking countries on the continent.

The Knowledge Society

When Marshall McLuhan articulated his vision of the global village in the 1960s, many answered with skepticism. Few would today. Indeed, the idea that all people share a common, inextricable fate and that they must share the world's resources in a safe, equitable manner is widely held in much of the world—and especially by those in non-industrialized, poor nations that make up the majority of the world's population.

Of course, a free, two-way exchange of information is essential to promoting democratic ideals and practices. For example, the Internet has been held up as a means to help Eastern European countries replace communism with new democratic identities. According to a 1995 report by the policy research group RAND: "The globe as a whole is 'shrinking' in the wash of information flows. The worldwide expansion of democracy may have less to do with how these technologies favor domestic democratic practices than with how they spread democratic ideals internationally." Some scholars suggest that increased Internet access can help stem the growth of potentially incendiary nationalism in Eastern Europe by giving children there broader exposure to other cultures. As Joseph Slowinski, an Indiana University scholar, wrote in *Educational Forum:* "Through this access, students can interact with school children from all cultures of the world, comparing these to their own. Through e-mail and web communications, students can explore the world."

Recognizing the importance of the Internet as a provider of information and education, the European Union (EU) has made the development of information technology in its new and poorer Eastern member states a priority. A 1997 EU report, *Towards a Europe of Knowledge,* declared, "We are now entering the knowledge society." In Eastern Europe, the large-scale efforts of governments and ministries of education have focused on building learning communities that will support the creation of a democratic culture, as mandated by EU membership.

The first Eastern European country to invest in a major information technology initiative for schools was Hungary, which introduced Sulinet (School Net) in September 1996. Sulinet aims to connect all Hungarian schools to the Internet by 2002. The total project cost: approximately $1.5 million. Other countries are following suit. The International Education and Resource Network (I*EARN)—a New York–based nonprofit—is working with educational, youth-service, relief, and development organizations to use telecommunications to build a "network of opportunities" involving students from more than 30 countries, including Albania, the Czech Republic, Poland, Slovakia, and others. For instance, I*EARN interns produce an online newsmagazine called *The Contemporary.* The staff reads submissions from students around the world and conducts editorial conferences via e-mail.

The World Bank, a major player in developing educational institutions, has tried to harness the power of the Internet for education in developing countries. During the 1997–1998 school year, it launched the

World Links for Development (WorLD) Program, which provides Internet service, e-mail, and multi-year training in the pedagogical uses of the Internet to students, teachers, and educational consultants in developing countries.

WorLD also helps build partnerships between schools and groups working in educational technology, provides telecommunications policy advice for the education sector in developing countries (for example, finding creative ways to reduce access and phone charges that hinder Internet usage), and evaluates the impact of Internet use in schools. Funding comes from public-private partnerships including corporations, non-governmental organizations, United Nations and relief organizations, and governments. By the end of 1999, 320 schools from 15 developing countries were "partnered" with schools in developed nations through WorLD. One WorLD program, entitled Our Human Environment, links several Canadian, South African, and Ugandan schools in online discussion groups and collaborative projects about natural habitats and questions of sustainable development in those countries.

In 1999, WorLD, I*EARN, and Schools Online joined forces to extend this global "community of learning" in a partnership called the Alliance for Global Learning. The alliance already links 30,000 teachers in more than 50 countries and hopes to bring more than three million students together via the Internet by 2005. As secondary students in Kampala work online with students in Toronto, an international community of learners is being established—one that may extend beyond their school years. Certainly such sharing of ideas—whether it takes place in the privacy of a young Kenyan girl's family home or in a secondary school classroom with 40 students taking turns at a computer—represents a significant step in the building of a global community.

Communities of Learning

Of course, the idea that learning communities can grow out of shared concerns, values, and ways of looking at the world is much older than the Internet. Organized communities are as old as human existence. Social groupings—whether they are defined as families, clans, ethnic groups, villages, towns, or nations—indicate the need for human beings to establish order and define their commonalities and differences. The same is true with groups organized around shared religious, cultural, and political values. Members of such groups might differ on interpretation of certain shared ideas and codes of conduct, but they are likely to cling to their core values, beliefs, and practices nonetheless. Educators trying to create international "communities of learning" via the Internet would do well to first determine the values and philosophic perspectives that might unite those groups of people together in the first place.

These communities might find multiple expressions for sharing experiences and information. A classroom teacher who wishes to explore the World Wide Web could begin, as I did, with certain key words. I chose "communities," "learning," and "education." Needless to say, I saw much that was not relevant to my search. But I also discovered a host of examples I didn't expect: Internet sites that promote the study of foreign language learning, online friendship clubs between students in different parts of the world, teacher education programs in Hong Kong, oral history projects documenting the lives of ordinary people in Brazil. Throughout the world, school systems and individual educators are investing time, energy, and expertise in the creation of learning networks and communities on the Internet.

One intriguing example of such online global communities is Globalearn, a Cambridge, MA, nonprofit that offers online "expeditions." Founder Murat Armbruster, a former journalist for United Press International, says he wants to prepare children "for global citizenship and responsible stewardship of the earth." Twice a year, Globalearn sends a team of explorers—teachers, photographers, journalists, and others—to some part of the world to document local environments and ways of life. These explorers post journals, research logs, and photos each day to the Globalearn web site.

When teachers and students visit the site, they might learn about the Mediterranean region or East Africa or Brazil. In the Explorer's Club, a moderated message board, they can post messages for the explorers. In a gallery, students can display their project-related work. Globalearn lets teachers customize an expedition to students' needs and interests, and teachers can choose materials and activities they decide are suited to their students' learning styles. This is an important feature of the site, and one that K-12 teachers might find useful, particularly given the vast amounts of information on the Internet.

The Internet also provides opportunities for teachers and students of foreign languages to improve their language mastery and improve cultural knowledge. Foreign-based web sites offer useful, current material for classroom exercises in the target language, as well as opportunities for online "chats" with native speakers in those countries. As Jean W. LeLoup and Robert Ponterio point out in *ERIC Review,* the education research magazine: "[Students] can readily see and comprehend that the language they study is . . . not just another subject to be studied in the confines of the classroom. Use of the target language takes on a real practicality when a student is attempting to converse with a native speaker over the Internet or is trying to find information that is available only on a local Internet site in a target language country thousands of miles away." The Internet is especially helpful for language teachers in isolated pockets of the United States and elsewhere in the world or those teachers without the benefit of foreign language colleagues in their school districts.

Sharing ideas—whether in a home or a secondary classroom with 40 students—helps build a global community.

Unfortunately, there is an unevenness in this global exchange. In Kenya and other African countries, for instance, three-quarters of the students have limited and poor basic education skills. So while the "digital divide" may be closing in richer Western nations, the promise of enhanced education and communication through the Internet is likely to remain a privilege of an elite few—those like Wanjiku in Nairobi—in poorer, less industrialized countries. Also, the information that children from poorer countries do consume originates largely from highly industrialized nations, and children from rich nations have less exposure to programs and cultures of poorer nations. New communication tools are helping create a global society, but the ideas and cultures of richer countries dominate this society. With the help of the Internet, Wanjiku may be able to experience life in France and Japan and the United States, but will kids in those countries be able to experience Kenya? And are they not poorer because of it?

More than 80 percent of all web sites are written in English, so non-English speakers automatically have a diminished access to the benefits of the Internet. German is the second most common web site language, yet it only comprises 1.6 percent of all sites, according to Slowinski. At least 60 percent of the Internet's host computers are located in the United States. Although many strides have been made in the non-English-speaking world in accessing the Internet, it is clear that the English-speaking world will continue to dominate conversation in cyberspace, a possible deterrent to bringing together those of different "tongues." Solving that challenge will be a great educational task for the 21st century.

For Further Information

S.L. Bryant. "Wiring an Asian Dragon." *Technos* 7, no. 4 (Winter 1998): 18–21.

S. Carlson and R. Hawkins. "Linking Students around the World: The World Bank's New Educational Technology Program." *Educational Technology* 38, no. 5 (September-October 1998): 57–60.

T. Gillespie. "Brazil's Museum of the Person." *Technos* 8, no. 2 (Summer 1999): 34-36.

GlobaLearn, 2 Tyler Ct., Suite B, Cambridge, MA 02140; tel: 617-492-8889; fax: 617-492-8887. **www.globalearn.com**

Intercultural E-Mail Classroom Connections. **www.iecc.org**

C. Kedzie. "International Implications for Global Democratization." In R.H. Anderson, T.K. Bikson, S.A. Law, and B.M. Mitchell, eds., *Universal Access to E-Mail: Feasibility and Societal Implications*. Washington, DC: Rand, 1995. **www.rand.org/publications/ MR/MR6650/mr650.ch6/ch6html**

J.W. LeLoup and R. Ponterio. "Using the Internet for Foreign Language Learning." *ERIC Review* 6, no. 1 (Fall 1998): 60–63.

J. Slowinski. "Implementing an Educational Internet in Central and Eastern Europe." *Educational Forum* 63 (Spring 1999): 204–208.

"Towards a Europe of Knowledge." Brussels, Belgium: European Commission, 1997. Online at **http://europa.eu.int/comm/education/orient/orie-en.html**

J. Woodell and J. Gray. "Exploring the Real World Online." *Technos* 8, no. 1 (Spring, 1999): 36–40.

World Links for Development (WorLD), World Bank Institute, 1818 H St. N.W., Washington, DC 20433. **www.worldbank.org/worldlinks/**

Teaching and Technology

A New Culture of Teaching for the 21st Century

To maximize the benefits of technological innovation, we need to change the way we think about teaching in K-12 schools

By Stone Wiske

Popular views of educational technology tend to exaggerate both its promise and its peril. Advocates tout computers and the Internet as instant remedies for dry curriculum and didactic instruction in schools. Alarmists worry that computers will replace teachers and that the World Wide Web will poison the minds of young people. Both extreme positions place too much emphasis on the technology itself. People—especially teachers—shape the impact of computers in schools more than the features of hardware and software. If we want to understand how to improve learning in schools, we need to pay more attention to the conditions affecting the culture and profession of teaching.

Certainly, interactive, networked, portable technologies have potential as educational tools beyond that of static materials like pencils and books, or broadcast media like radio and television. When used by knowledgeable teachers in a supportive educational context, these new technologies can significantly enhance teaching and learning.

Moving beyond "Plug and Chug"

The story of graphing calculators is an instructive example. These hand-held computers are becoming standard equipment in many U.S. mathematics classrooms. These advanced calculators have a small screen that displays mathematical functions in graphical form as well as in tables and formulas. They allow students to spend less time doing routine calculations, solving equations, and plotting graphs, and more time comparing mathematical functions, predicting the effects of variables, and making sense of representations of mathematical data. They are so inexpensive that many schools can afford to buy whole sets for their classes so that each student has one to use.

In recent years, mathematics textbooks have changed to incorporate calculator-based lessons, and the College Board has begun to permit students to use graphing calculators while taking the SATs. Teachers are gradually learning how to modify both the mathematical content of their curriculum and their approach to teaching to take advantage of these calculators. Some schools have equipment that links calculators to sensors for collecting data such as temperature, pH, movement, and light. The calculators can plot these data as a function of time and graph the results. They can also be connected to equipment that projects the work from any one calculator to a display so that everyone in the class can see it. In these ways, graphing calculators can support inquiry, thinking, and dialogue about mathematics and scientific data, rather than the "plug and chug" routines that have characterized U.S. mathematics classrooms.

What can we learn from this example about the conditions that enable technology to have important educational effects?

- First, the technology must afford significant educational advantage. In this case, calculators allow users to analyze mathematical information by manipulating linked representations such as formulas, graphs, and tables—an essential aspect of mathematical inquiry that is cumbersome with traditional tools of pencil and paper or chalk and blackboard.
- Second, the technology must be readily affordable, networked, and portable. As long as technology is expensive and difficult to move— like most computers—its impact in schools will be limited.
- Third, technology alone does not change school practice. Curriculum goals and materials, assessment policies, and teacher development must shift as well. Without these changes, a new technology will merely be used to enact traditional practices.

This last condition—changing the culture of education—is the most difficult to achieve. How did all these variables—texts, tests, and teachers—shift to support the integration of graphing calculators? Much of the impetus was provided by the National Council of Teachers of Mathematics (NCTM). This professional organization represents a wide spectrum of people interested in mathematics education: mathematicians, teacher educators, curriculum specialists, and classroom teachers. During the 1980s the NCTM worked collaboratively with all these groups to develop new standards for mathematics curriculum, pedagogy, and assessment. Several leaders of this movement had learned from the failure of the New Math reforms of the 1960s. This time they took care to build consensus with parents, teacher organizations, and policy-makers about the new standards.

The NCTM standards, issued in 1989, shifted the focus of the mathematics curriculum from rote rehearsal of isolated facts and formulas to investigating, communicating, and applying core mathematical concepts and habits of mind. Shortly thereafter, the NCTM issued complementary standards for the preparation of mathematics educators. In the ensuing decade, many state education agencies enacted compatible curriculum and assessment requirements. The National Science Foundation funded a series of "systemic" initiatives to support teacher preparation and development in line with the NCTM standards. Textbook publishers prepared new editions that reflected the new standards. This combination of initiatives supported concurrent changes in educational goals, professional development, and curriculum materials that were synergistic with the opportunity afforded by the new technology of graphing calculators.

Rethinking Traditional Teaching Patterns

This relatively encouraging story is not a cause for unbridled celebration, however. Despite the confluence of conditions supporting reform of mathematics education, U.S. classrooms have not changed quickly to resemble the NCTM ideals.

In their recent book *The Teaching Gap,* James Stigler and James Hiebert examine the results of the Third International Mathematics and Science Study (TIMSS), which compared mathematics and science achievement among fourth, eighth, and twelfth graders in 41 nations. The TIMSS data were collected in the mid-1990s, when the impact of NCTM reforms was only beginning to be felt in classrooms. Indeed, some have argued that these data should be regarded as a baseline against which to compare the results emerging from classrooms that enact practices consistent with NCTM standards.

Meanwhile, the TIMSS data are sobering. As Stigler and Hiebert put it, "The results are dramatic, and they do not paint a flattering picture of American education." Twenty nations, including Singapore, Korea, Japan, Canada, and France, scored significantly higher than the United States in eighth-grade mathematics. Only seven nations scored significantly lower than the United States.

Part of the study involved making videotapes of eighth-grade mathematics classes in three countries: Germany, Japan, and the United States. A panel of mathematics educators analyzed these videotaped lessons (and translated transcripts). The panel noted striking differences in the standard practices of the three countries. Japanese teachers typically engage their students in working on challenging problems, and then students share and discuss their solutions. Teachers of German students—whose scores were statistically comparable to those of U.S. students—typically lead students through advanced procedures for solving challenging problems.

In the typical U.S. lesson, however, students first watch their teacher solve low-level problems and then repeat the procedure on numerous similar problems. Whereas the tapes from Japan and Germany reveal that three-fourths of teachers develop concepts during a lesson, most U.S. teachers simply state concepts. The typical U.S. lesson places greater emphasis on memorizing facts and formulas than on understanding the underlying rationale. U.S. students usually follow the teacher's lead, while their Japanese counterparts spend much of their lesson doing challenging mathematics.

These patterns of pedagogy, Stigler and Hiebert conclude, are part of culturally embedded systems. Shifting classroom practice from routine rehearsal of skills toward higher-order thinking, independent inquiry, and sustained work on challenging problems is not a simple matter of introducing teachers to new technology or techniques. Learning to teach is less like learning to use a computer than like learning how to participate in family dinners: teaching is learned through watching and engaging in the approaches that one is expected to emulate. Pedagogical approach is bound up with a web of cultural assumptions. Each country has its own scripts for what happens in the classroom.

Enacting these scripts may include customary props or technologies. In Japan, teachers write copious notes on the blackboard as they explain concepts, producing a record of their main points that students can review. In contrast, the most common teaching technology in U.S. eighth grades is the overhead projector. U.S. teachers move on to a new transparency when they move to a new point. These technologies give students a different experience of the lesson: the Japanese blackboard offers a sustained and coherent picture, whereas the U.S. overhead projector provides an ephemeral and disjointed glimpse of the teacher's agenda.

Culturally embedded teaching patterns are difficult to change, but change is not impossible. Japanese teachers have made a major shift from the whole-class instruction and recitation that used to be their norm. Stigler and Hiebert report that this reform took several decades and required a systematic approach to educational change, including explicit learning goals for students, a shared curriculum, supportive administrators, and sustained efforts by teachers to make gradual improvements in their practice.

To change school practice, curriculum goals and materials, assessment policies, and teacher development must shift. Without these changes, a new technology will merely be used to enact traditional practices.

Stigler and Hiebert describe the Japanese system of change, which features school-based professional development focused on "lesson study." Groups of teachers meet over extended periods of time to develop, try out, and assess lessons. First the group defines a problem of practice and plans an approach to this problem in the context of a particular lesson, usually with a specific hypothesis in mind. Then the group members teach the lesson to their students and meet to discuss how it worked and how it might be improved. Once group members have developed an effective research lesson, they share it with other teachers. Because the entire country teaches the same curriculum, many teachers can benefit from this intensive study of a single lesson. Japan's new culture of teaching has developed through teacher-led research, collaboration, dialogue, and collegial exchange in the very schools where teachers work.

If we want new technologies to foster significant changes in the content and process of learning, we need to devise ways of changing the professional culture of teaching. Changing curriculum standards and materials, revising assessment devices and policies, supplying schools with technical infrastructure, and hiring appropriate technical personnel will all be necessary but not sufficient. We will also need to change the terms and focus of dialogue in schools to encourage talking about subject matter and learning. We will have to change the norms of professional collaboration so that observing colleagues, exchanging curricula, conducting rigorous classroom research, risking failure, and celebrating success become familiar patterns in school workplaces. Only then will teaching become a "true profession," as Stigler and Hiebert advocate, in which "the wisdom of the profession's members finds its way into the most common methods. The best that we know becomes the standard way of doing something."

How can we provide time for this kind of professional dialogue? In Japanese schools, the schedule is organized so teachers have time to meet with one another. Some U.S. schools have also redesigned their schedules so teachers can meet with colleagues to plan curriculum, exchange strategies, and analyze best practices. Educators are also exploring the use of new technologies to extend teachers' opportunities for collegial exchange about their subject matter and about effective practices. Stigler and Hiebert recommend that effective examples of classroom practices be videotaped, digitized, and annotated. A collection of such examples could allow teacher study groups to anchor their conversations in analysis of real classroom interactions. A one-hour video selected from the TIMSS tapes entitled "Eighth-Grade Mathematics Lessons: United States, Japan, and Germany" is now being used by professional development groups around the country.

It Takes a Cyber-Village . . .

The Internet offers a more interactive means of connecting teachers with multimedia resources, peers, and professional development leaders. For example, two web-based projects at the Harvard Graduate School of Education connect teachers and professional developers with research-based resources, teacher-designed curriculum models, and forums for collegial exchange. *Active Learning Practices for Schools* (ALPS) aims to support teachers in using educational approaches developed through research at Harvard's Project Zero. *Education with New Technologies* (ENT), developed at the Educational Technology Center at Harvard by faculty and graduate students, uses a research-based framework called Teaching for Understanding as a structure for integrating new technologies with practice.

The Teaching for Understanding framework guides educators to focus on four elements in helping students develop flexible and robust understanding, not just memorize facts and formulas. The elements are generative curriculum topics, clear understanding goals, performances that cause students to stretch their minds and apply their knowledge, and ongoing assessment using public criteria linked to goals. New technologies can enrich each of these elements; at the same time this framework helps educators clarify how to design and assess effective applications of these new tools.

ENT is intended to support collaborative groups of educators interested in using new technologies to support teaching for understanding. Designed around the metaphor of a village, this online environment includes a meeting hall where participants may confer, a resource library, a learning center offering online courses, and a gallery with detailed "pictures" of effective curriculum designs. The gallery incorporates lesson materials, student work, and reflections by teachers and students about the process of teaching for understanding. In the future, it will include video selections along with guides for study groups.

ENT also features a workshop where teachers can develop and discuss technology-enhanced lessons. Using the Collaborative Curriculum Design Tool, participants may work alone or with a team, communicating through an electronic message system that links to their e-mail. This interactive tool guides teachers to use the four elements of the Teaching for Understanding framework as they develop curriculum. Educators learn to develop generative curriculum topics—that is, topics that address important concepts in their subject matter, engage students' interests, and invite inquiry into related ideas. The tool also helps curriculum developers spell out specific goals for understanding: What exactly are students expected to learn, and why? Users then design a sequence of active-learning tasks that will enable students to meet those goals and demonstrate their understanding. Finally, the design tool supports the development of ongoing assessments that both improve and prove students' mastery of key goals.

Using this tool, educators are guided to apply new technologies in ways that enhance one or more of these elements of Teaching for Understanding. With this guidance, links to related resources, and an electronic communication system to support collegial exchange, the Collaborative Curriculum Design Tool enables educators to study and develop effective lessons, much as the Japanese teachers do in their study groups. Once teams test and refine a curriculum unit, they may publish it online so that others may replicate or adapt it. Shared units deal with a wide range of topics, such as developing literacy using web-based resources to communicate with local lawmakers and understanding the Pythagorean theorem through mathematical inquiry with software.

Integrating new technologies need not require radical change in educational goals and methods. Indeed, teachers often start by incorporating new tools into familiar practices. But even modest beginnings benefit from opportunities to see good examples, talk with like-minded peers and advisers, and gain easy access to resources.

In online learning environments teachers can surmount the barriers of time and distance to communicate, reflect, and collaborate with colleagues. As powerful, networked, portable computers become more readily available, these new technologies may help to foster the development of a professional culture among teachers. Such a culture of continuing inquiry into effective practice is necessary if we are to reap the potential benefits of new educational technologies.

For Further Information

Curriculum and Evaluation Standards for School Mathematics. Reston, VA: National Council of Teachers of Mathematics, 1989.

Professional Standards for Teaching Mathematics. Reston, VA: National Council of Teachers of Mathematics, 1991.

J.W. Stigler and J. Hiebert. *The Teaching Gap: Best Ideas from the World's Teachers for Improving Education in the Classroom*. New York: Free Press, 1999.

Third International Mathematics and Science Study (TIMSS). For information and reports, contact: TIMSS Customer Service, National Center for Education Statistics, Suite 311, 555 New Jersey Ave, N.W., Washington, DC 20208; tel: 202-209-1333; fax: 202-209-1679; e-mail: timss@ed.gov. **http://nces.ed.gov/timss**

M.S. Wiske, *Teaching for Understanding: Linking Research with Practice*. San Francisco: Jossey-Bass, 1998.

T. Blythe et al. *The Teaching for Understanding Guide*. San Francisco: Jossey-Bass, 1998.

Active Learning Practices for Schools (ALPS). http://learN.W.eb.harvard.edu/alps

Education with New Technologies (ENT). http://learN.W.eb.harvard.edu/ent/home/index.cfm

Preparing Teachers for the High-Tech Classroom

Teachers' unions, education schools, K-12 administrators, and government are scrambling to teach educators the technology skills many of their students already have

By Clorinda Valenti

When English teacher Stephanie Wilder was constructing her own web site for her students in grades 10 and 12, her frustration in trying to work with a software program to design a home page led her to appeal to a tech-savvy friend for help. "I felt like I was putting together a swing set and directions were written in an unknown language," says Wilder, a longtime teacher at Charlotte Country Day School in North Carolina.

Country Day is just beginning an initiative to make technology an integral part of curriculum and instruction. This transition has low-tech teachers like Wilder—who says she is still afraid to touch the VCR—working hard to learn how to use new technology in their classrooms and to explore how it might change their teaching styles. Now all teachers at the independent school are required to purchase IBM laptops, the cost of which is financed through the business office, and to report regularly to the principal on their use of software and the Internet in their classrooms.

When a school like Country Day makes the technological leap, a key requirement for success is teacher training and professional development. The late 1990s explosion in educational software and Internet resources has created an increased demand among teachers for guidance through a labyrinth of these competing teaching tools. Schools are challenged to devote more money and time to the effort. In addition, many leaders of the educational technology movement advocate a concomitant transformation of pedagogy and classroom management.

The number of computers in schools across the country doubled to 8 million between 1993 and 1999, according to a report from Market

Data Retrieval, the research arm of Dun & Bradstreet. And "Technology Counts '99," a national survey by *Education Week,* found that 97 percent of teachers use a computer for professional activities, 53 percent use software for classroom instruction, and 61 percent use the Internet.

But it is how teachers are learning to use the hardware, the software, and the Internet that concerns some educators. "We're asking teachers to fundamentally change the way they instruct and perhaps even the goals of instruction," says Barbara Stein, a policy analyst on technology for the National Education Association (NEA). She adds that teachers' preparation is a key predictor of whether classroom use of technology will improve student achievement.

Stein is concerned that school budgets are not allocating enough money for professional development in educational technology. According to the Technology Purchasing Forecast survey for 1999–2000, districts now spend only about 5 percent of their instructional technology budgets on professional development; the NEA recommends raising that figure to 40 percent. Besides more funding, teachers need more time to attend workshops and training sessions and to meet formally and informally with their colleagues to trade ideas and share successes and frustrations.

Stein points out that some schools still see technology as a separate strand from curriculum and instruction. The 21st-century school, she insists, demands a coherent schoolwide vision of how technology is aligned with educational goals.

Most teachers these days find themselves part of a schoolwide—or districtwide—shift toward the plugged-in and wired classroom. Since most training takes place at the local level, schools also must find the money, time, and experts for professional development programs in technology. Help has come from government agencies, businesses, policy-makers, school administrators, schools of education, and teachers' unions across the country, which have embarked on a myriad of initiatives to train teachers for the high-tech classroom.

The Clinton administration has made professional development one of the "four pillars" of its Technology Literacy Challenge. The federal government's role in teacher training has been to act as a stimulus by supporting model programs and providing seed money. A new federal grant program, Preparing Tomorrow's Teachers to Use Technology, will help universities and colleges to upgrade their teacher-preparation programs.

In addition, the Technology Innovation Challenge Grants program has directed $30 million to 20 model projects designed to develop teachers' technological skills. In El Paso, TX, thanks to Challenge Grant funding, 102 public school teachers in the Socorro Independent District have completed master's degrees in technology integration and, in turn, have served as mentors to another 568 teachers. Public schools in Olympia, WA, used the grant money to implement the Generation www.Y program, an 18-week course that teaches students in grades 6–12 to mentor their teachers to integrate technology into a curriculum-based project, lesson plan, or unit.

Local and state NEA affiliates offer diverse professional development opportunities, including conferences, workshops, trade shows, and mentoring programs. NEA also sponsors national events on technology, including an annual conference for educators interested in using technology to enhance learning. At the NEA's Focus on Technology web page (**www.nea.org/cet/index_educator.html**), teachers can find announcements of "virtual conferences," technology briefs, a message board, and a roundup of favorite software and web sites.

With the explosion in software and Internet resources, teachers need more guidance through a labyrinth of these competing teaching tools.

Teachers learning from one another is the focus of the 21st Century Teachers Network (**www.21ct.org**), a nationwide, nonprofit volunteer movement to encourage teachers to share their skills in using educational technology. There are now more than 11,000 registered users for the service, notes Sigrid von Abele, the site's Internet resource and content specialist, and 300–500 new users are signing up each month. The teachers are using the service to share ideas on curriculum, and plans are in place to establish mentoring programs through local chapters. "We are actively seeking Teacher Leaders to help organize chapters in additional subject, grade, and geographical areas," von Abele says. Sponsors of the initiative include the NEA, the American Federation of Teachers, and software and information businesses.

For the past 10 years the National Teacher Training Institute (NTTI), a project of 26 public television stations led by Thirteen/WNET in New York City, has been training teachers to use video, the Internet, CD-ROMs, laser disks, and other technologies in math and science instruction. Elementary, middle, and secondary school teachers in the program attend one- or two-day workshops at which master teachers demonstrate ways to create technology-based lessons that are interactive, explain and reinforce concepts effectively, and address various learning styles.

At a recent workshop, for example, a middle school science teacher demonstrated his "Sizing Seismograms" lesson, in which students go online to track real-time data to explore the geological power of the earth. The institute is based on a "teachers teaching teachers model," so graduates return to their districts to share the training, materials, and lesson plans with colleagues. NTTI estimates that 130,000 teachers will have received training through the program by the end of the 1999–2000 school year.

The institute has had a positive impact on the participating teachers, reports NTTI director Marsha Drummond. Program evaluations indicate that 80 percent of the teachers believe NTTI significantly improved their science and math instruction. The teachers' use of the Internet jumped from 30 percent to 80 percent. In addition, their ability to incorporate the Internet and video into math and science instruction climbed from 10 to 60 percent at the conclusion of the Institute to nearly 90 percent several weeks later.

While NTTI master teacher Ainsley Adams, a sixth-grade teacher at the Richard J. Bailey School in White Plains, NY, shares what he has learned with his colleagues, he relies on his school's technology coordinator for additional training in how to use the Internet in his classroom. Adams and his colleagues also take advantage of educational technology courses at the Edith Winthrop Teacher Center of Westchester in nearby Hartsdale. In New York State, 121 Teacher Centers, consortiums of public and private schools, serve as focal points for more than 100,000 teachers seeking professional development programs and credit-bearing graduate courses. Just across the Hudson River, the Rockland Teacher Center offers online courses in topics such as "Computers and Higher-Order Thinking Skills" and "Technology for Special and At-Risk Populations."

Despite the abundance of training opportunities, Adams says teachers at the Bailey School are constrained by a lack of computer hardware and Internet access: there are only two Internet connections for the school's 500 students in grades 4-6. Adams believes schools like his in economically strapped urban districts need to add hardware and Internet ports so that teachers can put their technological training to effective use. His observations are echoed in the *Education Week* survey, in which 69 percent of teachers who did not use the Internet cited a lack of "Net-connected computers" as the reason.

Teachers Train One Another

But what teachers need most is peer-to-peer instruction and mentoring, asserts Donald Blake, who analyzes trends in technology for NEA. This kind of professional development encompasses a range of activities from an informal sharing of tips through a web site to teacher-conducted workshops for fellow teachers. Formal training in peer instruction, however, usually is offered only at once-a-year state conferences, and the expense to the school of sending teachers for several days may be prohibitive.

Yet peer instruction is the method that educators prefer, Blake contends: "We've learned from numerous technology training sessions with state and local union leaders and members that the most popular training is that which is offered to them by their peers—classroom teachers we've enlisted to help us develop and facilitate training." Informal surveys and anecdotal evidence indicate that teachers find it easier to learn how to use technology from their colleagues because they too understand the world of the classroom.

In the Denver suburb of Aurora, CO, the Mission Viejo Elementary School has transformed itself, with help from the private sector, into a model program for training teachers to integrate technology into the curriculum. The school's 800 students have access to a computer center with 17 Macintosh computers, multimedia equipment, a scanner, a digital camera, and a video camera. Each classroom has from two to five computers, depending upon the teacher's level of expertise.

The business community has played a key role in training teachers to use the high-tech equipment, according to Mary McAuliffe, the school's technology curriculum specialist. In the absence of sufficient local and state funds for hardware and technology training, Mission Viejo has made a concerted effort to obtain grants and form business partnerships to advance its program. A major partner with the school, the US West Foundation—the charitable arm of US West Communications—provided free hands-on training in Internet use to Mission Viejo teachers.

McAuliffe believes that teacher training, to be effective, has to take place throughout the school day. To this end, she has created several innovative professional development efforts that involve both teachers and students. Eight teachers who have successfully integrated technology into their classrooms are designated as technology "coaches" for other teachers who are just learning the ropes. The focus of the coaching is to make the classrooms more interactive and to encourage students to be problem-solvers. In addition to day-to-day informal discussions, the coaches meet with their "coachees" for about an hour and a half every two weeks, while McAuliffe works with their students on technological skills. Coaches also are taken out of their classrooms four times a year for additional training.

McAuliffe helps teachers as needed and holds afterschool workshops where teachers can demonstrate projects on topics such as how to teach a concept or build a web page. About 60 percent of Mission Viejo teachers also take courses and workshops for credit through the district and local universities, and that figure is rising. "Teachers are being more proactive with technology training," McAuliffe reports. "The tough part of education technology is that there's no such thing as being trained—it's so dynamic. You're never on top of it all."

Students as Mentors

Some Mission Viejo students are helping their teachers with the new technology. Every teacher in the building has a "TechSpurt," as McAuliffe has dubbed them, fourth- and fifth-grade students who exhibit leadership skills and high motivation to work with technology. "They become mentors for the teachers," says McAuliffe. One TechSpurt helped a teacher develop an interactive multimedia production for a lesson on whale watching. Usually the TechSpurt will master the technical side of a lesson—in this case using HyperStudio, a multimedia authoring tool—and then help the teacher learn it. The program is very popular with students. Former TechSpurts who are now in middle school and high school even return to Mission Viejo on their vacations to work with teachers. A strength of the program, McAuliffe notes, is that it taps into students' knowledge of and comfort with technology: "Kids are raised with technology, and they're naturals at it."

Making students mentors for their teachers is but one way in which technology is changing the nature of pedagogy and professional development. Teachers may learn basic skills, such as how to use Windows or build a web site, but these skills must also be integrated into their teaching. The *Education Week* survey found that training on how to integrate technology into the curriculum has a greater impact on teachers than learning basic technological skills.

Although Country Day's Stephanie Wilder needed to work on her skills and even brush up on her typing, she says the more important challenge for her and her school is to explore new ways of teaching with technology. During and after the school day, Wilder and her colleagues can attend skills workshops given by the school's two computer experts. Meanwhile, the history and English departments have combined offices to encourage more interdisciplinary teaching. Wilder, who has taught at Country Day for 17 years, believes teachers should first determine instructional and student needs and then find the appropriate technology, instead of using computers and cyberspace as educational gimmicks.

Doug Clements, a professor of learning and instruction at the State University of New York at Buffalo, agrees with Wilder: "Many school structures have not changed for decades. Technology changes the culture of the classroom, the children, and teaching." As Clements sees it, systemic educational change has to occur before technology can be used effectively in classrooms. Schools need to do more than just train teachers to use new technologies: they need to rethink the structure of the school day, teaching methods, and the role of students.

"The success stories are in schools in which the local administrators support change and make serious attempts to get teachers to talk to each other," Clements says. Time can be set aside in teachers' schedules for talking with colleagues about changes in their subject area, for example. There should also be consistency in in-service training for teachers, not just a jumble of disconnected skills training. Clements suggests that principals work with local colleges or universities to present workshops on tech-related themes. He also sees mentoring of new teachers as crucial. "Teachers are caught in the crossfire with all the changes and expectations," he sums up. "What schools need is an ongoing systemic vision of how to integrate technology. This vision should be communicated with teachers, parents, and students."

According to the 1999 School Technology and Readiness (STaR) Report issued by the CEO Forum, a partnership of business and education leaders, professional development should focus on moving from traditional to new learning environments. Educators should move from teacher-centered learning to student-centered learning, from isolated work to collaborative work, and from factual, knowledge-based instruction to critical thinking and informed decisionmaking. The high-tech classroom should be more interactive and encourage active, exploratory, inquiry-based learning, as opposed to the didactic mode in which teachers feed students information. The report recommends that states develop standards for continuing education on integrating technology into the curriculum and that schools and districts establish proficiency standards and long-term plans for technology-related professional development. It also calls on schools of education to better prepare new teachers to use educational technology.

The CEO Forum is not alone in calling for schools of education to help prepare new teachers to use technology. Four states—South Carolina, North Carolina, New Hampshire, and Connecticut—now have technology training requirements for recertification, and 42 states require that teacher preparation include technology training. Although veteran educators may picture their younger colleagues as computer-savvy and ready to enter the high-tech classroom, the reality is quite different. *Education Week* found teachers who had been in the classroom five years or fewer no more likely to use technology than those who had been teaching for more than 20 years. Mission Viejo's McAuliffe has made the same observation in her school. She believes that schools of education are not doing enough to prepare their students to manage a classroom with technology. She would like to see increased innovation in preservice training, including more online degree programs.

At SUNY Buffalo, a six-month-old program leading to an Advanced Certificate in Educational Technology is intended to prepare new teachers for high-tech classrooms. The program offers graduate students in education interdisciplinary coursework in the social and psychological issues involved in using technology in the classroom, the use of computer-based technologies in particular subject areas, and the design and development of computer-based materials. "Technology training alone without a grounding in education theory and subject expertise is inadequate," notes Doug Clements, who teaches in the program. Students explore, for example, how learning theory interacts with the use of computers for instruction. They also learn how to be critical consumers of the software programs and web sites that will be competing for their attention—and school dollars—including a growing number of online opportunities to earn continuing education credits.

The quality of any training, online or offline, ultimately depends upon the people delivering it and their technological and pedagogical perspective. "What's more important than the teacher learning which switch turns on the computer," says NEA's Donald Blake, "is the encouragement and support from administrators and peers that builds the teacher's excitement about why the switch should be turned on in the first place."

For Further Information

Charlotte Country Day School, 1440 Carmel Rd., Charlotte, NC 28226; tel: 704-943-4500. **www.ccds.charlotte.nc.us/**

Focus on Technology. A web page by the National Education Association (NEA). **www.nea.org/cet/index_educator.html**

Generation www.Y. Dennis Harper, Project Director; tel: 360-753-8835. **http://geN.W.hy.wednet.edu/**

Mission Viejo Elementary School, 3855 South Alicia Pkwy., Aurora, CO 80013; tel: 303-693-0611. **http://missionpossible.ccsd.k12.co.us/**

National Teacher Training Institute (NTTI), Thirteen/WNET, 450 W. 33rd St., New York, NY 10001; tel: 212-560-2922; fax: 212-560-6992. **www.wnet.org:80/wnetschool/ntti/index.html**

"New Teachers and Technology" and "Technology in Education 1999," both by Market Data Retrieval, One Forest Pkwy., P.O. Box 907, Shelton, CT 06484-0907; tel: 800-333-8802; fax:203-926-0784; e-mail: mdrinfo@dnb.com. **www.schooldata.com**

Preparing Tomorrow's Teachers to Use Technology. U.S. Department of Education, 1990 K St., N.W., Room 6156, Washington, DC 20006-8526; tel: 202-502-7788; fax: 202-502-7775. **www.ed.gov/offices/OPE/PPI/teachtech/index.html**

Rockland Teachers' Center Institute, 65 Chapel St., Garnerville, NY 10923; tel: 914-942-2513; fax: 914-942-1805. **www.rockteach.org**

School Technology and Readiness. A series of reports from the CEO Forum on Education and Technology, 1341 G Street, N.W., Suite 1100, Washington, DC 20005; tel: 202-585-0208. **www.ceoforum.org/reports.cfm**

Socorro Independent School District, 12300 Eastlake, Socorro, TX 79927; tel: 915-860-3400. www.socorro.k12.tx.us

Technology Counts '99: Building the Digital Curriculum. A report by *Education Week,* 6935 Arlington Rd., Suite 100, Bethesda, MD 20814-5233; tel: 301-280-3100; fax: 301-280-3250; e-mail: ITO_STAFF1@ed.gov. www.edweek.org

Technology Innovation Challenge Grant Program, Office of Educational Research and Improvement, U.S. Department of Education, Washington, DC 20208-5544; tel: 202-208-3882; fax: 202-208-4042. www.ed.gov/Technology/challenge/

21st Century Teachers Network, c/o the McGuffey Project, 888 17th Street, N.W.,12th Fl., Washington, DC 20006; tel: 202-429-0572; fax: 202-296-2962; e-mail: info@mcguffey.org. www.21ct.org

US West Foundation, 1801 California St., Suite 1360, Denver, CO, 80202-2658; tel: 303-896-1266. www.uswf.org

Edith Winthrop Teacher Center of Westchester, 457 Hartsdale Ave., Hartsdale, NY 10530; tel: 914-761-6000; fax: 914-761-8854. www.greenburgh.k12.ny.us/wtc/wtc.htm

Commentary by David Perkins

"The big question is how to show up without showing up"

How can Internet technologies aid in professional development? We asked David Perkins, co-director of Harvard's Project Zero. He is the principal developer of ALPS (Active Learning Practices for Schools), a new web site designed to make Project Zero's "Teaching for Understanding" and "Thinking" resources readily available to schools. His reply:

I am interested in teacher development at a distance for a couple of reasons. First, there are a lot of good, powerful ideas about the practice of teaching that are not so widely adopted, and it would be wonderful if teachers had more opportunity to get acquainted with those ideas, shape them to their own needs and visions, and put them to work on behalf of learners. Second and relatedly, the pattern of educational practice remains fairly conventional. The reasons for that are complicated, but need for contact is one factor. Research shows that a rich process of professional development requires a lot of contact. It takes showing up. And not just showing up this weekend for a two-day workshop, but showing up again and again and again.

The big question is how to show up without showing up. The World Wide Web offers a possible way for professional development mentors to keep in touch with teachers or administrators on a fairly regular basis over time—to invite discourse, to suggest that they try new things, share their results, get reactions to their stories, both from the people offering this experience and from colleagues, and therefore nourish the process of development. There is some hope that distance education via the World Wide Web can help to crack this terribly tough nut of wide-scale teacher development.

The World Wide Web licks two problems in the process of trying to take teacher development to scale. One is an economic bottleneck. Given travel costs, program fees, and other costs, it's too expensive to show up all the time. The second bottleneck is one of expertise. Who is going to do this? Professional development requires a certain art and craft. A lot of the people with the knack and experience for it already are teaching and are not about to quit their jobs to go on the road. Now the nice thing about artful use of the World Wide Web is that they wouldn't have to do that. They could take part in web-based structures of dialogue as a sideline and stay where they are.

Your first thought might be that web-based professional development is second best to being there, and, in some respects, it is. Nonetheless, there are some surprising advantages. The web makes it easier to create a track record, because everything's written down, and tracing the development of interactions that take place with e-mail or online forums is good for research. Also, the web makes it easy for people to share their work with one another. Posting a case study from a teacher is easier than photocopying and distributing it to dozens of people. And electronically, there's almost zero cost to making such work available to everybody in the group.

We've also found that many teachers really value the asynchronous communication. They are busy and don't want to have to get together at a particular time. Even a group of teachers in the same school who, in principle, could sit down and have conversations with one another preferred to do most of their conversing online and asynchronously. Why? Because it is not always convenient to get together. Of course, some people feel less comfortable with asynchronous communication and having to translate their thoughts into a concise paragraph. They would rather sort out their ideas in conversation

Another thing we've learned is that an online course structure is a valuable way to move people along in professional development, more valuable than just offering examples and techniques via the web. Resources are good, but only the most self-directed teachers get around to using them. An online course offers structure that can keep people in motion. However, it's important not to go too far and turn an online professional development course into a purely academic experience. The important thing is to keep participants in the classroom, trying things, talking with one another and with us about what works and how, and discussing ways to improve.

Science: Venturing Online to Teach and Learn

As the list of impressive web resources for teaching and learning science grows, the role of teachers becomes more important, not less

By Alan Feldman

We are moving into a connected and digital world, and the signs are all around us. As adults, we are confronted daily with news about e-commerce, and many of us have recently made our first purchases online. We can't pick up a newspaper or magazine without seeing a string of web addresses, those cryptic letters starting with *www*, where we might learn more about a product, read more about a news report, or join a discussion group. At home, the majority of Americans are now accessible by e-mail; not long from now e-mail will be as universal as the telephone. Already many of our children routinely chat online while doing their homework. In schools, many students and teachers already have access to online resources from their classrooms, and national leaders promise online access from *all* classrooms by 2003. Increasingly, online resources for learning, work, and entertainment are replacing CD-ROMs and many uses of printed text: you may be choosing to read this article online in order to explore some of the web links as you read.

Without question, digital technologies are shaping our lives in profound ways. But there is reason to be skeptical about the impact of these technologies on teaching and learning. Students' need for support and guidance in their learning has not changed. Today's students may be surrounded by computers, digital information, and instant access to distant resources, but their need for interaction with adults who support their learning is as great as ever—and arguably even greater.

How will the astonishing power of this connected and digital world affect teaching and learning? To explore that question, I focused on science curriculum and looked at web sites that support effective learning and teaching in science. However, the ideas presented here are largely applicable to other domains of learning as well.

I used three criteria to select the sites listed below. First, the sites represent a range of purposes, including giving students and teachers access to distant sources of science content, making abstract concepts more visible and concrete through multimedia, making excellent science curriculum easily accessible, and transforming digital information to meet the learning style of the user.

Second, the sites demonstrate good design in their use of online technology. A well-designed site does not merely present lengthy text, but also utilizes web capabilities such as searching, linking, and viewing multiple representations.

Finally, the sites listed here are consistent with best practices for teaching and learning science. It is commonly acknowledged (if not yet common in practice) that good science teaching is inquiry based: rather than focusing on information, it focuses on questions that motivate learning. In inquiry-based science, students are directly involved in the adventure of *doing* science. The National Science Education Standards advocate inquiry into authentic questions—questions generated from students' experience—as the central approach to teaching and learning science. Many leaders in science education believe that high-quality online resources and online support for teachers are key components of any strategy for realizing this vision of inquiry-based science education.

One caveat is in order. Online educational resources suffer from the same instability as the rest of the online world: no one has yet figured out the economic models that will sustain these sites over time. At present, sites are supported by grants, advertising, corporate sponsorship, subscriptions, and government funding. Grant-funded sites have typically not yet tackled the issue of how to sustain themselves past the grant cycle. Sites supported by advertising have yet to become profitable, and there is a big question about the appropriateness of advertising on sites aimed at students in school. Sites paid for by corporations are supported only as long as the corporation's public relations group deems it in the company's interest. As for sites supported by subscriptions and by government, it is not yet clear whether they will attract enough subscriptions or interest for long-term survival. In short, "e-education" is in the same position as e-commerce: precarious, yet holding out great hopes for users. Yet the longevity of a site is important to teachers who may invest substantial time in learning how to use the resources with their students. The descriptions of online resources that follow include information on how a site is currently supported.

Access to Science Content, Including Multimedia

Good teachers have always known the importance of organizing the teaching of key concepts around questions of interest to students, and they have often found that traditional texts don't provide them with sufficient resources. The Internet allows teachers to download resources to use in their teaching, and students to download resources to use in research. This information may be text and photos, or it may be multimedia such as animations, simulations, and video clips. Free resources available online vary in reliability, but access to high-quality resources is getting significantly better. Just this past year, Encyclopedia Britannica (**www.britannica.com/**) put its entire database of articles online; at no cost, users can access the articles as well as multimedia clips and links to other online resources selected by experts.

Locating resources is easier online because the information is maintained in *digital* databases, which are searchable. Teachers and students can use the search capability, for example, to locate information about earthquakes in their state or the policies adopted by local and state governments to prepare for earthquakes. Most major newspapers, such as the *Boston Globe*, are available in online versions. At the *Globe*'s web site (**www.boston.com/globe**), a teacher or student can download the complete text of any current article and access limited information on articles going back to 1979 without cost; for access to the full text of an article from the archives, there is a charge. Science and health articles from the most recent week are available in a special section, from which they can be downloaded and saved.

Many government agencies have public education as part of their mission. NASA is at the forefront of government agencies in using online sources to reach the public, including teachers and students. Space Science News (**science.nasa.gov**) and Thursday's Classroom (**www. thursdaysclassroom.com**) are two sites, aimed at K-12 teachers and students, that provide information on current NASA research and related science content. Because of the multiplicity of NASA sites, it is helpful to use the search capability on the main NASA education web page (**education.nasa.gov**) to find information on a topic of interest across the full range of NASA-supported education sites.

ProQuest (**proquest.com**) and the Electric Library (**www.elibrary. com**) are subscription-based online services that allow subscribers to access the full text of current and past issues of hundreds of newspapers and magazines, as well as other content such as photographs and maps. Using ProQuest, a high school student or teacher can access the full text of articles in the magazine *Science* back to mid-1992, or an elementary school student or teacher can access articles in *Ranger Rick* magazine back to January 1997. Subscriptions to these services can be purchased by individuals, schools, or school districts. Many teachers view these services as essential to help students avoid the often futile Internet searching of public sites.

Today's students may be surrounded by computers and instant access to distant resources, but their need for interaction with adults who support their learning is arguably greater than ever.

Another subscription-based resource is Webivore (**www.webivore. com**), which has its own search capability that directs the user to carefully screened web sites. However, rather than leading to a simple list of sites, a search gives a student or teacher a preview that describes the content and scope of each site. The selection of sites and these previews are maintained by the Webivore content experts. Webivore also has a "Notebook" that lets users automatically create a bibliographic entry with the necessary elements, such as URL, name of the site, author, and date of collection. Webivore is a division of the Learning Company.

Online resources can allow the very latest news to become part of classroom learning. The Why Files (**whyfiles.news.wisc.edu**) is a free resource originally created by the National Institute for Science Education with support from the National Science Foundation, and is now supported by the University of Wisconsin–Madison Graduate School. Its mission is to explain the science and technology that underpin the news of the day and to make science understandable to the public. When the Mars probe disappeared, students were able to use the Why Files to locate background information on space exploration, its dangers, and the possible causes of the probe's demise.

Many science museums have posted exceptional multimedia resources online. The Exploratorium (**www.exploratorium.org**) has put a series of interactive exhibits online, including one called "Fastball Reaction Time," which uses the idea of a batter hitting a fastball to motivate thinking about how fast your reflexes are. Some displays are available only online, not in the museums themselves. For example, the Franklin Institute (**www.fi.edu**) has Benjamin Franklin's original armonica (a musical instrument made of spinning glass bowls) in its collection, but cannot let visitors play this fragile antique. Online, however, a digital simulation lets participants not only view the armonica but also play it and hear its distinctive sound.

Online Curricula

Collections of lesson plans designed for use by teachers are available online. To systematize access to these databases, the U.S. Department of Education funded the creation of the Gateway of Educational Materials (GEM; **thegateway.org**). From this site, a teacher can search multiple databases of lesson plans.

Teachers should view such plans with a skeptical eye, however. The first issue is that of quality: Who wrote the lesson plan? How well tested is it? And even if a teacher can locate a lesson of high quality, other issues remain. Databases of lesson plans may not describe all the relevant dimensions, such as the style of teaching and learning required by the lesson. Is the lesson based on reading and answering questions, or do students undertake their own investigation? What prior knowledge on the part of students (or teachers) does the lesson assume?

In fact, experience indicates that the individual *lesson* is not a very useful unit for communication among teachers. Fortunately, GEM's database also includes *curriculum units*, which cover longer periods of time, perhaps several weeks or months of study, so that teachers are more likely to be motivated to invest time in adapting the unit to their students' needs, their own teaching styles, and their district and state requirements.

Online curriculum units often provide links to additional online resources or activities. It is not surprising that some of the curriculum units that use online resources most effectively are found online themselves. However, there are substantial costs to creating, maintaining, and updating such sites, especially sites that include good support for teachers. The best sites typically have a person supporting teachers and students in their work and moderating discussions among students, teachers, and/or experts.

One very popular site—serving 200,000 elementary and middle school students—is Journey North (**www.learner.org/jnorth**), which describes itself as "A Global Study of Wildlife Migration." Journey North supports in-depth student inquiry by providing up-to-date information on the arrival of spring in the Northern Hemisphere. Weekly or biweekly updates on each species (e.g., manatee or monarch butterfly) and sign of spring (e.g., "leaf-out" or "ice-out") are based on local sightings reported by participating students, satellite tracking, and experts. Teachers are supported through online forums and a detailed, well-organized curriculum guide that is available online. Journey North, run by a small staff, is currently a free site, supported by the Annenberg/Corporation for Public Broadcasting Projects, with a commitment to continue funding through 2003.

Like Journey North, OnLine Class (**www.onlineclass.com**) is distinguished from other sites that offer curriculum units by its attention to teacher support. OnLine Class runs approximately nine separate units concurrently; these units are appropriate for a range of subjects and grades. Each unit provides resources for project-based learning, links classes to one another via e-mail for exchange of ideas, and hosts online displays of the work of each class. Recent science-related courses have included Physics Park (in which classes explore the principles of physics by designing a roller coaster) and Blue Ice (an exploration of the food web or weather in Antarctica). The cost per class is $300 per 10-week session, and the site is run by a small staff that serves several hundred K-12 classes in any given session.

One Sky, Many Voices (**onesky.engin.umich.edu**) was created at the University of Michigan to provide innovative, inquiry-based weather curricula for K-12 classes. Activities are designed for collaboration among classes at different schools. Support for teachers is very strong. This is an excellent example of a web site that can be personalized for a particular class. Just as in the commercial world a web site can be personalized to fit your own viewing habits (such as providing the news on topics of interest to you or the current price of your favorite stocks), this site can be personalized to give announcements specific to a class—for example, it may announce that a hurricane or other extreme weather condition is approaching their area and tell the class what to look for. One Sky, Many Voices is funded in part by a grant from the National Science Foundation.

Science Brainium (**usa.brainium.com**) includes science content and activities for students and teachers, K-8. The site has grown rapidly and is already very popular in schools in Canada. For teachers, it offers curriculum units (including easily printed worksheets) and plans to add discussion forums. For students, it presents information in text and as interactive multimedia, including a magazine and an extensive "edutainment" area—all with science-specific content. Funded by venture capitalists, the site is supported by subscriptions at $70 per class per year; subscriptions include permission for teachers and students to access the site from their homes.

WhaleNet (**www.whalenet.org**) is an ideal place to find a range of resources about whales and other marine mammals. Through satellite tracking of miniature transmitters attached to animals, students are able to follow individual animals and conduct research about their migratory paths. Marine mammals serve as the theme around which teachers can organize lessons in math, science, the environment, and technology— though the creation of these links is largely left to teachers using the site's excellent resources. This site is free, and is currently supported by the National Science Foundation.

Tools for Teachers

Online sites provide tools that support teachers in making resources available to their students, matching curriculum to national and state teaching standards, and keeping current by communicating with peers.

Some sites provide tools with which teachers can create and post their own curriculum resources to guide their students. Of particular note is Knowledge Network Explorer (**www.filamentality.com**), which has several tools for teachers. One tool, "Filamentality," supports teachers in selecting a goal and then choosing a format—including "Hot Lists" (annotated links) and "WebQuests" (structured web-based research activities). The site makes it possible for teachers who know nothing about designing web pages, and perhaps are not experienced curriculum designers, to design a curriculum unit and set up their own online resources through a very simple, non-technical process. Knowledge Network Explorer also includes "Blue Web'n," a selection of exemplary web sites to which teachers can create links as they develop their own student activities. Knowledge Network Explorer's tools are a project of Pacific Bell's Education First program. Similar sites include nschool.com (**www.nschool.com**), SchoolNotes.com (**schoolnotes.com**), and Blackboard.com (**www.blackboard.com**). SchoolNotes.com is supported by advertisers; nschool.com is supported by corporate partners but does not show the corporate logos on any page accessible by students; and Blackboard.com is supported by its parent company and has no advertising or corporate logos. All three of these sites make use of the Web's ability to disseminate information flexibly, quickly, and cheaply.

Online tools are just now emerging to support teachers in their use of national and state standards for teaching. Standards documents, including those for science, can be accessed in many states through interactive software. For example, teachers in Massachusetts can download a tool called the Curriculum Library Alignment and Sharing Project, or "CLASP" (**www.massnetworks.org**), a searchable database containing the Massachusetts Frameworks that is designed to assist teachers in correlating content and standards. There is also a related database of sample lessons submitted by teachers, correlated to the various standards; access is restricted to the contributing districts.

At Science NetLinks (**www.sciencenetlinks.com**), designed specifically for K-12 science educators, teachers can locate lessons, online resources, or benchmarks (national standards), searchable by grade level and topic area. The online resources are all selected after review by a panel, and a few of the best are designated as Educational Super Sites. The lessons use these reviewed online resources and are keyed to specific benchmarks. Science NetLinks is a project of the American Association for the Advancement of Science and is part of the MarcoPolo partnership sponsored by MCI WorldCom.

The Hub (**ra.terc.edu/alliance/HubHome.html/**) provides teachers, curriculum specialists, and principals with online resources to support educational reform goals in science and mathematics. The site is maintained by the Regional Alliance for Math and Science Education at TERC, a nonprofit research and development organization in Cambridge, MA. Up-to-date information about science standards for every state and for national organizations is found here. Listservs are an important tool available at this site; these online discussions conducted by regional "networks" of local and state educators allow teachers and others to exchange ideas or pose questions. Topics of these listservs include Curriculum, Instruction, and Assessment (including Science); Equity; and Informal Education. The work of the Regional Alliance is supported by the U.S. Department of Education.

Recommendations

Online resources have undergone enormous development in the few short years that the Internet has been widely available. While we don't yet know how online sites will be supported financially in the years ahead, there is every prospect for continued improvement of these already strong resources and online curricula as developers gain experience in weaving together access to digital information, including interactive multimedia, curriculum resources, and tools for teachers. The experience of teachers and students using these online resources will be essential to help the developers "get it right."

At a recent meeting of about 25 developers of online web sites sponsored by the Genetic Science Learning Center of the University of Utah, there was a widespread sense that the art of creating online resources for students and teachers is still in its earliest phase of development, analogous to a Model T Ford rather than a modern automobile. Nevertheless, there has been some serious research on the experience of teachers using these resources that points to some clear recommendations for the use of online resources in the teaching and learning of inquiry-based science:

Use the Internet to broaden the context of locally grounded inquiry.

While students can now learn about almost any topic using the Internet, teachers should be careful to anchor the initial investigations in students' own hands-on activities—using real materials that they can pick up and manipulate—so that the concepts involved become comprehensible and meaningful and are not just abstractions. As students engage with a subject, teachers can use Internet resources to extend their learning. Using Journey North resources, teachers engage their elementary students by planting tulips and observing when they first emerge. When students have collected their own data, they can see how their data fit into a larger set of data collected by many classes across the country. Online communities are an excellent way for students to place their own work in a larger context, thereby deepening their learning.

Select online curricula with multiple entry points for content, pedagogy, and technology.

Teachers who attempt to learn how to use new technologies while also making significant changes in their curriculum and pedagogy need support for their professional growth. To provide such support, some online curriculum units offer tutorials in teacher guides, online training workshops, and access to telephone and e-mail help lines. However, professional development that focuses on the technology itself is not enough. It must also focus on *content* (background information about the science concepts) and on *pedagogy* (how to teach this content through inquiry-based activities).

Teachers who have successfully made shifts in their teaching to incorporate these interrelated changes report that the shifts may take three to five years to complete. Online curricula should have entry points that reflect the content needed by the students, the pedagogy understood by the teacher, and the technology available in the school, so that as teachers use the units in successive years, they are able to weave in the new and challenging content, pedagogy, and technology more fully.

Help students locate educationally productive Internet resources.

One of the most common arguments for connecting schools to the Internet emphasizes the benefit of giving students access to a vast fund of information. At sites such as ProQuest or Electric Library, students can access up-to-date publications that formerly were available only at research libraries. Too often, however, when students attempt to find information on the Internet, they get in over their heads, finding little that is relevant to their topic or appropriate to their level of knowledge.

Good online curriculum points younger students to preselected web sites that extend their level of understanding. There are online tools that make this simple for teachers to do. By middle school, many students have become skillful readers and are able to locate good online resources themselves. Teachers should provide structure for their work by being certain that each student has a clear goal in mind.

Use data to deepen students' inquiries.

Good science teaching makes use of data—both data collected by students and data collected by scientists. First, students need a reason to analyze data—a question they want answered. Second, data sets should be kept very simple—students are most successful with simple counts (e.g., birds that appear at the feeder, individuals with attached or detached earlobes). Third, teachers should work with the data themselves before giving them to students—an obvious point, but one often overlooked. Finally, teachers should avoid giving "recipes" for data analysis and should instead emphasize the roles of judgment, hypothetical thinking, and critical reasoning in examining data.

Choose online curricula with robust curriculum design.

Teachers should be careful to select online resources that match the level of the school's (and class's) infrastructure. Asking students to download and view satellite photographs through a 28.8K baud modem is a sure way to generate frustration. And even in districts with excellent technology, fast networks, and good technical support, teachers experience days when the network is behaving poorly or the server is down. Or, if everything is working fine in your school, the classroom with which you are collaborating is having some of these problems—or a snow day!

The best online curriculum units have a robust design that make use of technology and the Internet only when the technology deepens the learning for students. When using technology, robust curriculum design includes local sources of data that the computer can access (e.g., key documents downloaded in advance, CD-ROMs, or data stored locally) to supplement online data. Robust curriculum design does not limit itself to classes with advanced technological capacity, but supports those that have a wide range of technical capacity and knowledge. It typically includes activities that do not use technology or that take place offline.

Use the power of digital media to reach the full range of learners.

Digital media can give a major boost to students with distinctive learning needs. Students who cannot access information presented as text have multiple options. If their limitation is visual, they can read the text in large type or listen to the text read by the computer. If their limitation is in comprehension of text, they may have the option of viewing rich visual or multimedia representations of the information. Similarly, students who have trouble keeping lab journals because of writing impairments can dictate their journals using speech-recognition software.

Teachers remain key to students' learning.

We are fast approaching a time when there will be extensive, impressive online resources for teaching and learning science. Despite these emerging resources, however, the role of teachers is becoming more important, not less. My own recent research study concluded:

> Although there is strong evidence that the Internet can provide resources to support good teaching and learning, there is no evidence that it can replace the role of teacher and peers. Our research and experiences indicate the opposite: The universe of information has grown larger and more complex because of the extraordinary capabilities of new technologies. As a consequence, students need more than ever the guidance of experienced and skillful teachers to learn to their full potential.

The prospect of ever-better online resources for science education will help skillful teachers come closer to the goal of reaching all their students with inquiry-based science content that reflects the world in which students are growing up.

The author wishes to thank Pam Buffington and Bob Coulter for their helpful comments and suggestions on an earlier draft of this article.

For Further Information

A. Feldman, C. Konold, and B. Coulter. *Network Science, A Decade Later: The Internet and Classroom Learning.* Mahwah, NJ: Erlbaum, 2000.

"Report of Proceedings: Science Education on the Internet." Salt Lake City, UT: University of Utah, Genetic Science Learning Center, 1999. **www.genetics.utah.edu/webmeeting/**

D. Lyons, J. Hoffman, J. Krajcik, and E. Soloway. "An Investigation of the Use of the WWW for On-line Inquiry in a Science Classroom." Paper presented at the Annual Meeting of the National Association for Research in Science Teaching, Chicago, 1997.

National Research Council. *National Science Education Standards.* Washington, DC: National Academy Press, 1995.

E. Soloway and R. Wallace. "Does the Internet Support Student Inquiry? Don't Ask." *Communications of the ACM* 40, no. 5 (1997): 11–16.

Math: Calculating the Benefits of Cybersessions

Math teachers and students eager for fresh ideas or a few helpful tips are discovering that help is just a few keystrokes away

By Gene Klotz

The spread of web-based communications in the 1990s has sparked a revolution in teaching and learning. This is especially true at the college level, but it is increasingly applicable to K-12 schools, too. In mathematics, as in other disciplines, the Web is expanding our concept of the classroom itself, changing what gets learned and how, affecting the student-teacher relationship, and providing access to new resources.

Although use of e-mail has been common among college faculty since the mid-1980s, more and more of us are communicating via web pages, not only among ourselves but also with our students. We use web pages to present syllabi, homework assignments, and other information about our courses and ourselves; to spark lively and learning-filled online discussions among our students; to assign and receive homework, and even to administer homework and tests; to communicate teaching materials; and to deliver the content of entire courses.

There is a great effort to make the World Wide Web more available in schools, yet its educational role remains clouded by questions such as what to do with this resource, how to make it available, and how to restrict what is available. As the Web becomes a more familiar fixture in homes, it may become a tool for students' educational activities and parents' involvement with education—when it isn't being used for accessing the NBA home page and other entertainment sites, that is.

We need to figure out, in addition to how to get more schools wired, what the Web's unique contributions to education can be and how to prepare teachers to take advantage of this resource. At this time it is often hard to find what you want, hard to verify what you find, and just plain bewildering. The Web changes daily: like Topsy, it just grew. And yet, its educational potential is enormous.

What have we learned so far?

On the Web, each person is a potential publisher.

Teachers, students, parents, and administrators can present their own ideas, their teaching and learning strategies and materials, for all the world to see. In doing so, they are creating an enormous body of educational material, with a great deal of chaff but also some very nourishing wheat. It is possible to publish graphics, animations, even videos and sound, as well as multicolored text. In all subjects this diverse potential can serve the needs of different types of users—although when overdone it can be distracting.

Enterprising teachers all over the world are using the Web to publish their own classroom materials. To see what a splendid medium the Web can be, take a look at these online examples of lessons by math teachers, which are as pedagogically useful as they are attractive:

- Suzanne's Mathematics Lesson by Suzanne Alejandre, a teacher at the Frisbie Middle School in Rialto, CA, and a Math Forum associate. Web site: **forum.swarthmore.edu/alejandre/**
- Fibonacci Numbers and the Golden Section, a fun site that includes puzzles and problems, produced by Ron Knott, a visiting fellow in computing at the University of Surrey in England. (Fibonacci lived in Italy during the Middle Ages and helped introduce the Hindu-Arabic number system to the West.) See **www.mcs.surrey.ac.uk/Personal/R.Knott/Fibonacci**
- Cynthia Lanius of Rice University publishes K-12 math lessons at **math.rice.edu/~lanius/Lessons/**
- Cathleen Sanders, a high school teacher in Hawaii, teaches an interactive online geometry course, Connecting Geometry. See **www.k12.hi.us/~csanders/**
- For wonderful examples of student work, browse through the ThinkQuest Library: **www.thinkquest.org/library/**

The Web makes the world a classroom.

The boundaries of traditional communications have been shattered by the Web. E-mail and online discussion groups allow everyone to communicate with a wide range of people. In addition to reaching friends and acquaintances, you can easily connect with people you don't know but with whom you share an interest.

Every day, several hundred students from around the globe send questions to our feature, "Ask Dr. Math," usually from their home computers. Around 10,000 students a week participate in our half-dozen "Problems of the Week," often for school assignments or as special projects. Tens of thousands of teachers, students, and others search through our "Web Math Library" for material to use in class or to further their understanding.

Students from classrooms all over the world are involved in joint projects, such as using the method of Eratosthenes to measure the circumference of the earth (for a fine example, visit **k12science.stevens-tech. edu/noonday/noon.html**).

The Web offers mentoring and tutoring for both teachers and students.

At the Math Forum, discussion groups exist on a wide variety of subjects. For instance, one visitor entered the question: "How has your school used computers to improve instruction in mathematics at various levels from Algebra I through Calculus?" Another asked what parents could do to help their kids learn math on the Web. Another wrote: "Our school is looking at the place of critical thinking in the curriculum. Can anyone help me with information about critical thinking and mathematics?"

Teachers and students may be able to find mentors who are willing to help them achieve their learning goals, such as figuring out how to deal with a teaching problem or mastering a subject. The Math Forum has a number of mentored projects that are among our most popular features.

Students (and sometimes teachers) e-mail questions to "Ask Dr. Math" (**forum.swarthmore.edu/dr.math**), and an army of talented, trained, and cheerful volunteers write back. The goal is not so much to give students answers as to help them find the answers themselves. For example, take the following exchange from the Math Forum:

```
Date: 01/11/2000 at 14:59:11
From: Jennifer
Subject: word problem with cubed

The edges of one cube are 2 cm longer than the edges of
another. The volume of the smaller cube is 152cm less
```

than the volume of the larger cube. Find the lengths of the edges of each cube.

I've got the 3 equations: Vs=x3; Vl=(x+2)3; Vs+152=Vl

Vs being the volume of smaller cube; Vl being the volume of larger cube

Then I substituted everything in and got:
    x3+152=(x+2)3

Where do I go from here? I've done this problem over and over and haven't been able to figure it out. I know that the answer is 4cm and 6cm but I need to know how to get there. Please help.

~~~~~~

Date: 01/11/2000 at 16:18:29
From: Doctor Rob
Subject: Re: word problem with cubed

You've made a great start on this problem. Everything you've done is correct so far. Next, expand $(x+2)^3 = x^3 + 6*x^2 + 12*x + 8$, bring everything over to the right-hand side, and combine like terms. You'll get an equation with only one positive real root, which is the answer for x.

~~~~~~

Date: 01/11/2000 at 17:57:20
From: Jennifer
Subject: word problem with cubed

Thanks for helping me get this far, but I'm still stuck. I did what you said and I got $0= 6x^2 + 12x - 144$.

What do you mean when you said "You'll get an equation with only one positive real root." If I square root all the numbers I get no whole numbers but 12 and 6^3 or 4^3 don't equal it.

~~~~~~

```
Date: 01/12/2000 at 10:17:41
From: Doctor Rob
Subject: Re: word problem with cubed

Divide both sides of the equation by 6:

 0 = x^2 + 2*x - 24

Solve this either by factoring the right side into two
factors, or by using the Quadratic Formula. There are
two values of x which work in this equation. One is
positive, one is negative. You should reject the nega-
tive solution as being physically meaningless in the
context of your problem. The remaining answer is the
one you seek.
```

Teachers often make class projects from the Math Forum's various "Problems of the Week." Categories include elementary, middle school, geometry, discrete math, trigonometry, and calculus (see **forum. swarthmore.edu/pow**). Many students send in their solutions just for the fun of it. Mentors review these answers and respond, perhaps suggesting how the students might improve their work or, if they have correctly solved the problem, an alternative approach they might try.

To help teachers with questions of pedagogy, the Math Forum offers "Teacher2Teacher" (**forum.swarthmore.edu/t2t**), where presidential awardees and other highly qualified persons discuss teachers' questions. We plan to start a similar service for individuals soon. Here is a typical exchange, this one about incorporating writing into math class, between a teacher and a "Teacher2Teacher" mentor, Gail:

```
Question: Do you have students write in math class
(i.e., journal writing, step-by-step explanations of
how they solved problem)? What do you think the bene-
fits are of having students write about math? How do
you think students feel about having to write in math?

Response: I have my fifth graders keep a reflection
journal. In it they tell me at least one thing they
"learned" or were curious about at the conclusion of
a lesson. These journals take just a few minutes to
```

write, and then I ask each group to share their ideas
with one another. I wondered when I started using them
if my students would fuss. Fifth graders can be whiny
sometimes. Surprisingly, when I forget to ask them to
take a moment to reflect, someone invariably reminds
me. I look over what they have written and try to jot a
note or two on each page. That does not take me long,
and I get a glimpse at what they learned (sometimes it
is a real eye-opener for me!).

Mentored environments provide opportunities for meaningful communication and focused support and feedback. Imagine you're the only
teacher of a particular course in your area. Whom do you go to for advice on specific problems you may have? The online environment enables teachers to link up with other teachers in similar situations or with
potential mentors. One teacher wrote to an online mentor following a
helpful exchange on the Math Forum: "Thanks for e-mailing me back
with the information. I wasn't expecting that or all the other helpful
hints that have come in as a result of my query. I don't feel so alone anymore in my search."

The Web creates immediacy, linking lessons to day-to-day events.

Current real-world material is available on the Web to give classes an
immediacy that can't be found in textbooks. For example, J. Laurie
Snell, a retired professor from Dartmouth College, combs leading newspapers for stories that make use of probability and statistics. Abstracts
are published on the Chance web site (**www.dartmouth.edu/~chance/**),
along with discussion questions for use in class.

To practice other quantitative skills in a real-world environment, you
can choose a hurricane from a database stretching back for some years,
"run" the hurricane to see its path, its velocity, even a simulation of what
it would have looked and sounded like at a site of your choosing (see
www.logal.net/test/data_v5/earthpulse/disaster_center.html).

Web sites of professionals can make their work accessible, and sites
exist in fields from architecture to zoology. Government agencies such
as NASA (**www.nasa.gov**) and the Census Bureau (**www.census.gov**)
also have much to offer math instructors and students.

The World Wide Web is a new and revolutionary educational tool: it
is a tool for lifelong learning, both for students and teachers; it offers

schools access to an incredible wealth of resources; and it provides special opportunities for developing partnerships between communities and their schools, for better communication between schools and parents, and for more effective local and corporate involvement through mentoring and other interactive volunteer service.

As is the case with any tool, the Web is not an end in itself, and it can be abused. Its effective use in schools requires that communities help their schools sustain and enhance what is already working well in education with new online possibilities. The future will require skills that students and teachers need to practice now.

How to Find Useful Web Resources

The amount of information on the Web can be overwhelming. The Web is an environment in which teachers and students are challenged to make sense out of the chaos, learning their way and carving paths suited to their own particular needs. The multiplicity of web pages and points of view includes urban legends, spoofs, and the just plain incorrect. However, this unevenness itself creates chances to cultivate critical faculties in evaluating arguments and material—and the Web is being so used by some teachers.

Public discussion forums offer multiple perspectives (often conflicting) that have to be interpreted. Some people have not yet learned how to converse properly on the Web: some lack civility, some monopolize conversations, many forget to make a meaningful subject line, or post to an inappropriate thread of the discussion. Nonetheless, the Web offers much of merit and great opportunities to obtain the input of others and to develop ideas through broad-based discussions.

Fortunately, there are a number of sites that carefully review the material they list. For example, at the Math Forum we have reviewed all of the 5,700 pages in our "Web Mathematics Library" (**forum.swarthmore.edu/library/**). Sites that review material in all subjects include two federally sponsored projects: the Gateway to Educational Materials, or GEM (**www.geminfo.org**), and the Eisenhower National Clearinghouse for Mathematics and Science Education (**www.enc.org**).

Even on a trusted site that reviews material, the sheer quantity available can seem overwhelming to the inexperienced. The Math Forum has organized its links for many common topics; for example, go to our search page (**forum.swarthmore.edu/grepform.html**) and search for *pi* or *tessellation*.

To better help teachers, students, and parents, we at the Math Forum are exploring the development of "local" Math Forums that would tailor a collection of resources to fit the specific needs, goals, and standards of a given school or district, taking into account socioeconomic conditions and other local variables.

History: Mining for Gold in a Mountain of Resources

A Library of Congress project shows the promise of online resources for teaching and learning history

By Bill Tally and Melissa Burns

At Dow High School in Midland, MI, students in Michael Federspiel's social studies class pore over congressional transcripts from a 1913 water rights hearing involving the city of San Francisco and Yosemite National Park. As part of their study of the conservation movement in the American West, they also review political pamphlets by John Muir and other contemporary advocates on both sides of the issue.

At Williamsburg Middle School in Arlington, VA, students studying the Civil War take the role of Civil War journalists and analyze dozens of period photographs from the studio of Matthew Brady.

And at University Library High School in Champaign, IL, students use oral histories of Depression-era immigrants as models for the oral histories they collect from immigrants in their own community.

All these students are conducting their research at the Library of Congress—thanks to the American Memory collections, the library's new online archive (**memory.loc.gov**). American Memory comprises more than 40 primary-source archives, each including hundreds or thousands of documents, photographs, pamphlets, films, and audio recordings from U.S. history and culture. For the first time, students from all parts of the country and at all grade levels are working with the raw material of U.S. history right at their desktops.

There is now an abundance, even an anarchy, of sources and materials available to teachers and students via the Web. This means teachers and students need whole new sets of skills to use the material in meaningful ways.

To support teachers and librarians in using these new digital resources effectively in the classroom, we and our colleagues at the Education Development Center in Newton, MA, have worked with the Library of Congress to develop the American Memory Fellows Program (AMF), a national staff development project. Each year, the program brings together 25 teams of middle and high school teachers and librarians from around the country to develop, test, and publish innovative classroom activities that use the online primary-source collections.

The program has three phases. During a six-week online orientation in late spring, Fellows get to know one another, and the digital collections, through web-based activities and discussions. At the week-long AMF Summer Institute in Washington, DC, in late July, Fellows become immersed in the collections, explore methods of inquiry using primary documents, design their own humanities lesson, and begin to act as "critical friends" for one another. During the following school year, the Fellows try out, observe, and revise their humanities lesson in their own classrooms. Through the use of electronic portfolios, they share and reflect on their developing expertise with colleagues online.

Learning to Filter

The project emerged from classroom research in which we found that students using primary sources as a major part of their study began to exhibit more of the traits we associate with good historical thinking: they posed questions, observed details, and began to speculate about what was going on *behind* the documents, to get at the all-important issue of context. And we found that for teachers and students the new technology broadened access to primary sources enormously.

But we also discovered that using digital archives poses a new set of problems. In the past, teachers and students relied on "expert filters" such as librarians, textbook publishers, and professional historians to help them find good, relevant material. The new media have done an end-run around all kinds of expert filters. The resulting universe of information is wider and richer, but it is also more varied: you can find oral histories of the Depression and discussions about Toni Morrison's novels, but you can also find advertising, sex, and endless web sites dedicated to dubious cultural trivia.

Schools and teachers accustomed to the problem of scarce information now face a quite different challenge: an overabundance of information. More than ever, teachers and students need help sorting out which parts of this new landscape are relevant to questions or problems they have, how to locate useful texts, how to read and evaluate them, and how to apply what they have found to their questions or problems.

Working with American Memory, teachers learn that the criteria that make a humanities resource valuable include authenticity and open-endedness. Do the resources give students access to voices, perspectives, and conflicts that can deepen their understanding of a historical or cultural phenomenon? Do they encourage students to be active interpreters and meaning-makers?

Yet even when digital resources are authentic and open-ended, like those in American Memory's primary-source archives, their sheer volume and variety require students and teachers to develop and use new skills.

Accordingly, one of the goals of the project is to build "information literacy," which has at least two major components. First there is the practical part: how to navigate around the technology to find materials—using search engines to locate documents, and scanning them quickly to determine their relevance. Second and even more important are the evaluation skills: Where did this document come from? Can I rely on it? How useful is it to my purposes?

For example, middle school students often approach the impressive collection of selected Civil War photos looking for images of life and death on the battlefield. Usually they are surprised to find virtually no images of battlefields massed with soldiers; rather, the battlefields are strangely empty. Why? Linking to background information on the collection, they learn that Matthew Brady's cameras were too cumbersome to allow the kind of journalistic coverage that would evolve later.

Learning to Ask Why

They do find plenty of pictures of the aftermath of battle, including famous images of Confederate dead at Gettysburg, Antietam, and elsewhere, with captions like "Bodies of Confederate dead gathered for burial." How trustworthy are these as data about the war and how it was fought? Again, students must consult the background information to discover that most of the photos were taken by photographers traveling with Union troops and presumably sympathetic to the Union cause. Thus, while the pictures portray many details of the battlefield faithfully (dress, weaponry, landscape), students can see that they also narrate a particular perspective on the events—that the Confederate cause is a lost one and that these soldiers died in vain.

Finally, if they are guided by a good teacher, students can become fascinated with the hundreds of images of mundane camp life in the Civil War—and here the real value of the collection becomes apparent. These more prosaic pictures make visible many aspects of the war that are frequently overlooked in conventional histories, such as the important role of black "contrabands" (runaway slaves seeking protection behind Union lines who were often put to work at menial tasks).

In trying to figure out whether the contrabands were well treated and what impact they had on the progress of the war, students are investigating authentic questions with no clear-cut answers. They need to closely examine the visual evidence of the photos—How are the black men and women positioned vis-à-vis the white soldiers? What jobs are they doing? How well are they dressed?—and consult other primary and secondary sources for additional information. Through exercises like these, we hope students will develop the habit not simply to think like historians, but to be lifelong critical thinkers, able to gather and weigh evidence.

Evaluation skills are especially important when teachers and students deal with historical archives. Online archives are unedited and can pose challenges for teachers, in part because they let students see the ugly side of U.S. history, including racist and sexist language that most of us today find offensive. In 19th-century political pamphlets and newspapers, for example, there are often stereotyped portrayals of African Americans, immigrants, and women. Many teachers are not adept at talking about these sensitive issues in class so they need skills for working with this material, for teaching students ways to approach it with a critical eye.

As teachers develop information literacy, they become able to do some of the filtering themselves by assembling well-chosen sets of materials to suit their pedagogical aims. For example, at Pleasant Valley High School in Chico, CA, social science teacher Brett Silva has set up a historical role-play for his students that involves a provocative set of primary sources from the 19th century. The students are asked to mediate a Texas land dispute between Native Americans and white settlers. The primary-source documents present the issue from an Indian perspective, a white perspective, and a 19th-century Quaker perspective. Brett uses web resources to help his students understand that human history is contested and that it reflects multiple points of view. He invites his students to see how the world was and how it might have been different.

The American Memory Fellows Program and others like it are building communities of reflective practitioners who are using the new resources and sharing their experiences. Currently, our community consists of 150 educators who are assembling an archive of teacher-tested materials that is available on the American Memory home page. The Library of Congress hopes that the collection of lessons will serve not only as a source of excellent curriculum materials, but also as a model for how teachers can use the vast archives to develop units on their own.

Other Valuable Nuggets

These online resources can give a boost to humanities teaching and learning:

EDSITEment (**www.edsitement.neh.gov**), the "gateway" site of the National Endowment for the Humanities, brings together what its creators call "the best of the humanities on the Web." The designers have selected valuable online resources for teaching English, history, art history, and foreign languages, and have surrounded them with lesson plans and in-school activities. The 49 web sites featured are rich in content, and the lesson plans are well-written. Educators can also sign up to participate in in-school activities that reinforce and recognize learning through the Internet, using the EDSITEment resources. There are good parent activities on this site as well.

History Matters (**www.historymatters.gmu.edu**) is indispensable for high school and college teachers of U.S. history survey courses. The site offers resources such as first-person primary documents that focus on ordinary lives and require students to actively analyze and interpret evidence. Created by scholars and teachers at the American Social History Project of the City University of New York and George Mason University's Center for History and New

Media, the site mostly covers the period from 1876 to 1946, though more materials are added regularly.

The Valley of the Shadow (**jefferson.village.virginia.edu/vshadow2/cwhome.html**) is an excellent resource for studying the issues behind the Civil War in vivid detail. Developed by Ed Ayers and his colleagues at the University of Virginia, this archive contains thousands of primary resources documenting two Shenandoah Valley communities on different sides of the Mason-Dixon line. Ideal for student documentary research, the site offers census records, newspapers, photographs, government papers, letters, and diaries, as well as overview documents that orient the researcher in time and place. The site includes online lesson plans for teachers and a variety of other aids for student research.

The federally sponsored AskERIC project (**ericir.sunsite.syr.edu**) has a virtual library of more than 1,200 lesson plans for teachers on a range of K-12 topics, from language arts lessons such as spelling and phonics to social studies topics such as the Oregon Trail and the U.S. Postal Service. In addition, the AskERIC Q&A service promises to answer teacher questions about educational theory or practice within 48 hours using a nationwide network of experts and databases of the latest research.

K-12 teachers will find a rich variety of arts-related lesson plans, curriculum units, and activities at the Kennedy Center's ArtsEdge Curriculum Studio (**artsedge.kennedy-center.org/cs.html**). Elementary lessons include teaching traditional Japanese songs and learning the history and art of making African masks. One high school curriculum unit explores the theme of monsters in literature, music, and drama.

For Further Information

American Memory Fellows Program (AMF), Library of Congress, 101 Independence Ave. S.E., Washington, DC 20540; 202-707-5000. **http://memory.loc.gov/ammem/ndlpedu/amfp/intro.html**. AMF teaching units created by Fellows can be viewed at **http://memory.loc.gov/ammem/ndlpedu/index.html**

Literacy: Charlotte's Web Meets the World Wide Web

As new technologies change how we communicate, what effect are they having on how we teach and learn to read and write?

By Julie M. Wood

In a second-grade classroom near Boston, I watched two eight-year-olds create their own classroom newspaper. They used a template from a publishing software product to create the banner, and selected the two-column format. Then they imported digital photographs of teachers and children in their school and added captions below each image. Earlier that day these same children had listened to their teacher read a (printed) Russian folk tale aloud to the class, exchanged handwritten notes on scraps of paper, and checked their e-mail messages. They navigated seamlessly from one medium to the next without hesitation, understanding literacy in ways that were difficult to imagine 20 years ago.

New technologies are dramatically altering the way we communicate. We routinely exchange information and meanings through images and sounds as well as texts—often in some combination of all three. So it should come as no surprise that fundamental changes are taking place in the way experts define the nature of literacy instruction in the 21st century. The pressing question facing researchers and practitioners in the field of literacy: How can we help our students develop the literacy skills they'll need in this rapidly changing high-tech society?

Is literacy still defined as the ability to produce and understand printed text? Should it be more than that, given the ease with which we can combine video and photo images with whatever we produce on our word processors? Assuming we ever agree on a new definition of literacy, how then will we measure literacy skill—a question necessitated by our current emphasis on standards and high-stakes assessments?

New technologies mean that students have more resources at their fingertips in the form of electronic and online texts. Computers and other high-tech gadgets offer multisensory opportunities for learning. That is, students can access ideas in multiple ways: by seeing, hearing, manipulating objects, and recording their voices. These capabilities can be particularly valuable for learning-disabled students, who often benefit from multi-modal learning strategies.

For younger children, new software such as National Geographic Atlas of the World or Encarta Africana allows students to interact with their texts. A student who is stumped by a word—What does it mean? How do I pronounce this?—can get an answer immediately through text, voice replication, and pictures. This offers a potential solution to a lack of prior knowledge, which researchers have identified as a fundamental reason why some students fall behind grade level in reading. By building on students' knowledge base—or increasing their knowledge base quickly and efficiently as they learn to read—interactive media promise to help level the playing field for students who come into reading instruction already two strikes down.

Researchers Charles Kinzer of Vanderbilt University and Donald J. Leu Jr. of Syracuse University contend that knowing how to access information quickly from multiple data sources is one important literacy skill that children will need to learn. Finding the best sites that contain useful, accurate information while ignoring irrelevant or inappropriate material poses a real challenge. But locating information is only the beginning. Learning to separate the wheat from chaff will become increasingly important since a single keyword search for "Phantom Menace" may produce more than 3,000 matches. Students, say Leu and Kinzer, will need to become proficient in asking meta-analytic questions such as: What is the best information for my purposes? How can I tell? Has this person [the author] reasoned well? Practitioners can help them do this by giving very specific instructions, as well as by modeling methods such as "think alouds"—vocalizing what they as more sophisticated researchers would do.

Once students have mastered these skills, they must learn how to synthesize information from a variety of sources into coherent ideas, and then to communicate those ideas in the appropriate way. In classrooms of the future, students will need to become savvy about selecting the appropriate tools to express themselves. For instance, in a multimedia culture, where color video, sound, and hypertext are all readily available communication tools, does it still make sense to make the analytic essay the centerpiece of high school writing instruction? With e-mail and word processing, do different writing styles and formats now need to be taught?

Part of literacy training will be to teach students how to draw on the expertise of others, according to Leu and Kinzer. If students do not personally know how to design web sites, edit video, and create cohesive narratives for their multimedia presentations, practitioners can teach them to tap into "distributed knowledge"—that is, to figure out who knows what and how to learn from them. In this way, sophisticated new tools and rapid advances in software products will allow them to draw on experts' knowledge rather than trying to become experts themselves in everything.

We have amassed a robust research base, which we can use to reconceptualize literacy instruction in the 21st century. Why start from scratch when we already know so much?

The question of what to teach is accompanied by one just as urgent: how to teach. How can literacy instructors take advantage of the multiple forms of information and presentation that multimedia offer? At all grade levels, Internet workshops, collaborative multimedia projects, e-mail, and online chat rooms are changing the way students interact with each other—i.e., students teaching students. Young children may follow along with stories as they're read aloud and innovate changes to the stories with writing and art tools. Middle school students can write and illustrate their own interactive stories using multimedia tools and share them with their class. Electronic porfolios allow older kids to access each other's stories and make comments, giving a more public face to their work. For all students, word processing makes revision—which research shows is a key practice for improving writing skills—less daunting.

My research focuses on exemplary teachers whose primary concern is how best to teach students to read and write. For one study, three primary-level teachers at two schools near Boston allowed me to observe them in action throughout a school year. All three have reputations as excellent teachers of reading and writing. They are also innovators, developing strategies for integrating new technologies into their reading and language arts curricula.

In no way did using computers turn the children I observed into the academic automatons that techno-critics like Neil Postman seem to fear. In fact the opposite occurred; as I watched, children worked together more than they normally would to write stories, search the web, or create multimedia presentations. The computers served as gathering places where children could show off their works-in-progress, such as a presentation about Martin Luther King Jr. using Kid Pix's multimedia tools, or share their latest discoveries, such as a web site with Japanese folk tales written by children their age. Publishing software enabled students to make posters, reports, or picture books based on what they were learning, and presenting what they know in a good-looking format boosted their motivation.

The Historical Perspective

Postman is not alone in expressing concern about the effects of new technologies on literacy. A glance through history shows that the shift in emphasis from the spoken to the written word concerned both Socrates and Plato. Socrates predicted that the written word would make people "cease to exercise memory because they will rely on that which is written." Plato argued that "no man of intelligence will venture to express his philosophical views in language, especially not in language that is unchangeable, which is true of that which is set down in written characters."

Postman asserts in *Amusing Ourselves to Death* that Plato's objection foreshadows the 20th-century shift "from the magic of writing to the magic of electronics." He warns that electronics are transforming our way of thinking and the content of our culture, and turning students into isolated, individual problem-solvers. In his 1994 book *The Gutenberg Elegies*, literary critic Sven Birkerts laments that printed books will eventually be devalued, despite their potential to expand our horizons and nourish our souls. In other words, thoughtfulness involves more than the consumption of information.

Gavriel Salomon of the Hebrew University of Jerusalem expresses similar concerns. In a 1997 article for *Phi Delta Kappan*, he predicts that new technologies will encourage children to capture quick sound bites of information, rather than conducting meaningful, in-depth explorations. Because visual media are less abstract than unillustrated texts, comprehending stories via movies and videos is less of a cognitive challenge, he warns. However, according to Salomon's earlier research, adults may be able to stimulate children's cognitive development when viewing electronic material by giving them a learning objective. Salomon's observations have vast implications for parents and educators who will use media to help children derive more meaning from a range of text presentation formats.

The issues identified by Postman, Birkerts, Salomon, and others provide a much-needed counterpoint to the wide-eyed optimism of technology mavens. However, it is worth noting that while children now have unprecedented access to mere information, it is also true that school systems are holding teachers accountable for developing students' higher-order thinking skills, such as summarizing, evaluating, and contrasting ideas. The age of the automatons is not upon us quite yet.

Furthermore, Seymour Papert of the Massachusetts Institute of Technology has demonstrated that well-designed software that encourages abstract thinking can, in fact, *accelerate* children's cognitive development. Computers, he writes, are "objects to think with," allowing kids to explore, experiment, and express their ideas in ways that would be more difficult without this tool.

What Can We Learn from Research?

Unlike those in some fields where a relatively strong research base supports educational technologies (e.g., science), members of the literacy community are far from reaching consensus on how new technologies can best enhance literacy development. Leu writes in a forthcoming article in the *Handbook of Reading Research* that, as yet, we have little empirical data because hardware and software—and their use in schools—change so quickly. Moreover, few of today's researchers manage to conduct experimental studies and publish their work in traditional journals before it becomes obsolete, he writes.

In addition to rapid change and a slow publishing cycle, I see a more profound reason for the paucity of research: the collision of two very different cultures. The literacy community has a culture all its own. Although nearly all its members use technology for their own writing and research, at heart many members are still a bit technophobic. Suspicious of new classroom tools to enhance reading and writing instruction, they are reluctant to give up the print-based research questions and methods that have served them well. A quick glance through the International Reading Association's catalogue reveals only one book about educational technology. Similarly, at the 1999 the National Reading Conference, I noticed very few reports of literacy research involving educational technologies.

Similarly, techno-enthusiasts have their own culture. Many are convinced that since technology is here to stay, we ought to find ways to use it everywhere, including all areas of education. But when they begin to design educational tools, techno-enthusiasts often fall back on the outdated teaching styles they grew up with, such as behavior/response, rather than incorporating new constructivist theories about learning by doing. Herein lies the paradox: most current software products are far from what a literacy expert would desire. Excellent software would entice them to conduct research about how such products can help children learn to read and write. But unless ideas from the two fields can cross-pollinate, the teaching tools will not satisfy literacy experts.

How can we bring the two cultures together? The first step is to get literacy experts and software developers to really talk to each other. For example, in one of my courses, I set up conversations among students with vastly different ideas about using technology to support literacy instruction. I pose such questions as: How would you use technology to set up a publishing center in your classrooms? What would be the pedagogical considerations? What would be the implementation issues?

In their 1996 study, "Learning in Wonderland: What Do Computers Really Offer Education?" Salomon and Harvard's David Perkins describe several innovative technology-based programs that are closely aligned with current research in psychology and pedagogy that could serve as models for the future. Many of the applications they endorse focus on collaborative, often multidisciplinary e-mail exchanges among students that are designed to foster knowledge networking. This "networking pedagogy" involves "genuine and purposeful knowledge construction and design, thus inviting understanding performances and high-level thinking," they write.

The online conferences sponsored by BreadNet of Middlebury College are a good example of multidisciplinary networking. They enable high school students to exchange essays, questions, and ideas about books such as Anne Frank's *Diary of a Young Girl* or *To Kill a Mockingbird.*

Resources that Work

Since such novel applications of technology are often not commercially available, they have received less mainstream attention than products such as Davidson and Company's Reading Blaster, which offers a game-like format and heavy doses of drill-and-practice.

Searching out the best software and web sites for children and devising lesson plans that emphasize serious thinking and a focused approach to research becomes even more challenging for practitioners who want to combine good literacy instruction with new technologies.

My own research has shown that much of the currently available software is not pedagogically sound. For instance, software that supposedly teaches vocabulary may have kids simply match definitions to words. Without presenting words in multiple contexts, students' understanding of those words is limited to the narrow context suggested by the software—preventing students from truly "owning" a word in all its multiple nuances and meanings, which vocabulary experts say is necessary if students are to actually feel comfortable using new words.

In general, commercial developers bring a business orientation to developing software; I have first-hand experience as an educator brought on board at the very end of a project to retrofit sound educational goals (impossible) or provide a stamp of approval (unethical). For example, a company may incorporate NASA space footage that's spectacular and free and makes an attractive-looking product. Then they'll go back and try to attach some educational value to the footage, treating educational substance as secondary to the product's stylish look.

The more sophisticated applications are not commercial but rather are developed in university settings and think tanks, such as the Center for Applied Special Technology. Developers of such products are usually content to reach a niche market, and profit is a secondary consideration. Students may learn French by helping hapless "Philipe" find an apartment in *à la raconteur Philipe* (developed at MIT) or examine artifacts from ancient Greece via the Perseus Project (developed at Harvard). PBS's new reading and storytelling show *Between the Lions* is an example of an appealing TV program and accompanying web site that is built around a fundamentally sound, research-based curriculum. Such programs and products that offer the right balance of scaffolding and easy-to-use-tools are especially beneficial.

In devising innovative strategies for using new educational tools, we need to draw heavily upon what research says about good teaching using traditional methods. The literacy community has amassed a robust research base over hundreds of years, which we can mine as we reconceptualize literacy instruction in the 21st century. Why start from scratch when we already know so much about effective strategies?

Still a Place for Paper

The idea of electronic books, or "e-books," is still highly experimental, and several issues need to be resolved before we take an e-book to the beach or the hammock. First, e-books can be expensive. Second, resolution of text is still poor. Third, as Princeton historian and e-book proponent Robert Darnton told the *New York Times*: "One thing that seems to be missing is paper, the feel of a book when you hold it, its grain, its texture, its elasticity, its whiteness. The sensation of paper is bound up in the experience of reading. We have a long-term kinetic memory of paper."

Though some, like literary critic Birkerts, find the whole notion of reading e-books offensive, future generations raised on digital texts will likely embrace them. Innovative thinkers such as Don Tapscott, author of *Growing Up Digital*, point out that members of what he terms the "Net Generation" will quickly acquire fluency with such innovative tools.

Computers don't exist in a vacuum. How they are used should be closely matched to the instructional needs of teachers and the learning styles of a particular group of students. There are no one-size-fits-all solutions to the intelligent use of new tools. As ever, children need to have extensive exposure to printed texts and spend time reading them and being read to. A world in which a well-worn copy of *Charlotte's Web* or *Green Eggs and Ham* goes unread is unthinkable. And as we move forward with electronic books and hand-held electronic writing devices, we must remember that the ultimate goal of reading is to be able to understand and interpret a wide range of texts, and the ultimate goal of writing is self-expression and communication regardless of the delivery system. Although these ideas seem self-evident, I am often surprised at how seldom they are mentioned in our national debate about the future of learning.

It is fairly safe to say that the Net Generation will have its own ideas about how to best use digital texts, communication devices, and the capabilities of computers and artificial intelligence beyond what we can imagine today. The Net Generation will regard what we now describe as mind-boggling innovations as the commonplace tools of reading and writing. Ten years from now, today's discussions about the pros and cons of technology will seem as quaint as Plato's fear that the written word would implant forgetfulness in men's souls.

For Further Information

Between the Lions. PBS series. www.pbs.org/wgbh/lions/index.html

S. Birkerts. *The Gutenberg Elegies.* Boston: Faber and Faber, 1994.

Book Raps. Australian web site of book discussion groups for elementary students. http://rite.ed.qut.edu.au/oz-teachernet/projects/book-rap/index.html

Book Reviews. Children can read book reviews written by others and post their own. www.i-site.on.ca/booknook.html

BreadNet, Breadloaf School of English, Middlebury College, Middlebury, VT 05753. www.breadnet.middlebury.edu/blsefiles/BLSEBnet.html

B.C. Bruce. "Literacy Technologies: What Stance Should We Take?" *Journal of Literacy Research* 29, no. 2 (1997): 289–309.

Center for Applied Special Technology (CAST), 39 Cross St., Suite 201, Peabody, MA 01960; tel: 978-531-8555; TTY: 978-538-3110; fax: 978-531-0192. www.cast.org

S. Christian. *Exchanging Lives: Middle School Writers On-Line.* Urbana, IL: National Council of Teachers of English, 1997.

J.W. Cunningham. "How Will Literacy Be Defined in the New Millenium?" *Reading Research Quarterly* 35, no. 1 (2000): 64.

M. Kamil. "Computers and Reading Research." In D. Reinking, ed., *Reading and Computers: Issues for Theory and Practice.* New York: Teachers College Press, 1987.

D.J. Leu Jr. "Technology and Literacy: Deictic Consequences for Literacy Education in an Information Age." In M.L. Kamil, P. Mosenthal, P.D. Pearson, and R. Barr, eds., *Handbook of Reading Research III.* Mahwah, NJ: Erlbaum, 2000.

D.J. Leu Jr. and C.K. Kinzer. "The Convergence of Literacy Instruction with Newtworked Technologies of Information and Communication." *Reading Research Quarterly* 35, no. 1 (2000): 108–125.

D.J. Leu and D.D. Leu. *Teaching with the Internet: Lessons from the Classroom.* Norwood, MA: Christopher-Gordon, 1999.

N. Negroponte. *Being Digital.* New York: Random House, 1995.

S. Papert. *Mindstorms: Children, Computers, and Powerful Ideas.* New York: BasicBooks, 1980.

S. Papert. *The Children's Machine.* New York: BasicBooks, 1993.

S. Papert. *The Connected Family: Bridging the Digital Generation Gap.* Atlanta, GA: Longstreet Press, 1996.

D. Perkins. *Smart Schools.* New York: Free Press, 1992.

D.N. Perkins. "Why We Can't Let the Technological Tail Wag the Pedagogical Dog." *Education Bulletin* 40, no. 2 (June 1996): 32.

N. Postman. *Technopoly.* New York: Random House, 1992.

N. Postman. *Amusing Ourselves to Death.* New York: Penguin, 1995.

The Read In! Event 2000. Web site for students and authors to celebrate children's literature. **www.readin.org**

G. Salomon. "Of Mind and Media: How Culture's Symbolic Forms Affect Learning and Thinking." *Phi Delta Kappan* 78 (January 1997): 375–380.

G. Salomon and D. Perkins. "Learning in Wonderland: What Do Computers Really Offer Education?" In S.T. Kerr, ed., *Technology and the Future of Schooling.* Chicago: University of Chicago Press, 1996.

J.H. Sandholtz, C. Ringstaff, and D.C. Dwyer. *Teaching with Technology: Creating Student-Centered Classrooms.* New York: Teachers College Press, 1997.

D. Smith. "Is This the End of the Story for Books?" *New York Times* (November 20, 1999): A15–A17.

D. Tapscott. *Growing Up Digital.* New York: McGraw-Hill, 1998.

J.M. Wood. "The Teaching of Vocabulary by Computer Software: A Content Analysis." Unpublished qualifying paper, Harvard Graduate School of Education, Cambridge, MA, 1997.

Managing Technology

A Tech Coordinator's Road Map for the Information Highway

Some advice for K-12 schools that are starting or overhauling technology programs

By Shelley Chamberlain

When my daughter was a senior in high school, she desperately wanted her own car. As fate would have it, her favorite cousin took pity on her and gave her a car he was planning to sell. She was delighted—now she had her independence. In her euphoria, however, she failed take into account all the hidden costs of operating that car. She (or in this case her parents) had to pay to insure the car and maintain it in operating condition.

This car analogy comes to mind when I think about using technology in our schools. As with my daughter and her car, the costs of using technology in schools are not immediately obvious. And unless we plan for both the financial and the human costs of running and maintaining the technology, it will not get us where we want to go.

The Lexington, MA, public school system, where I work, has a population of 5,807 students taught by 481 full-time and 235 part-time professional staff. The school system has six elementary schools, two middle schools, and one high school, which along with the town offices and library are part of a townwide area network (now built with coaxial cable but soon to become fiber).

Like most towns in Massachusetts, Lexington developed a five-year technology plan for the schools, which was approved by the state's Department of Education in 1994. Thanks to limited state monies and a long-term financial commitment by the town's taxpayers ($6 million to date), Lexington has a robust infrastructure. Our school system has 1,200 networked computers, with every classroom, library, and school office connected to our network.

Our car is road ready and the gas tank is full. Although I certainly do not have all the answers, I have learned these eight driving lessons in an effort to help keep our school system's technology program on the road and heading in the right direction.

1. Have a general and detailed road map

A three- or five-year technology plan for the system is a necessary road map. In Lexington's case, we needed a five-year plan to qualify for state technology funds. Plotting the route requires much time and energy, but you need to know both where you want to start and where you want to end up.

In 1994 we made a plan to distribute technology resources. We deliberately chose to put most of the resources into the elementary classroom. At the end of five years, we planned for each elementary school to have five computers per classroom, at least five computers in the library, common areas of access for specialists, and a lab of at least 13 computers. To provide technical and curricular support, we assigned a part-time technology facilitator as well as a part-time instructional technology specialist. Elementary curriculum specialists and librarians in each school were to provide some technological support as well. At the secondary level, where there are many different departments and courses, using technology is much more complex. Our elementary road map did not fit, and we are still developing the map appropriate for that level.

The best way to plot a technology road trip is to develop system-wide goals—the starting point and the destination—but also to have detailed plans by site. For example, create one detailed itinerary for the elementary schools as a unit, one for the middle unit, and one for the high school.

2. Make a system-wide commitment

The fiscal and administrative leaders of the school system and local government must make a commitment to a long-term technology plan for the schools. Just as one does not set out on a long trip with half a tank of gas, the drivers of technology—the teachers—need to be assured that their use of technology in the classroom will be fully supported and sustained. Most school systems are tempted to do too much at once, but they need to realize from the beginning that technological support must be a priority for many years. Maintenance and renewal are a lifetime commitment.

We have demonstrated this commitment by convincing the town to provide the funds to consistently upgrade software and hardware and to allow us to offer relevant professional development. By honoring our commitment, teachers can be confident that their efforts to learn how to use new technologies will pay off.

3. Agree who will drive—and where

Commitment from the top is not enough; the end-users must make a commitment as well. Teachers need to persevere in the use of technology. In Lexington, an elementary task force has worked to identify places where technology is essential to support the elementary curriculum. We have agreed on units in which to make technology-enhanced lessons an integral part of the curriculum.

For example, in a first-grade unit on shelters, technology-enhanced activities are embedded in some of the lessons. Every first-grade teacher is now expected to teach these integrated lessons. An added benefit of these units is that students will gain technological skills (such as word processing or using a database for research) while doing the activities in the unit, rather than as isolated skill sets.

4. Develop resources to match common agreements

At Lexington, we make decisions on how to distribute technology resources in the same way we select any curriculum materials: through a committee of teachers who work with a curriculum specialist or department head. Once we've identified units where technology offers clear and compelling benefits toward addressing key curricular objectives, those units must be supported with appropriate resources, both financial and human.

For the first-grade unit on shelters, the committee and curriculum specialists evaluated several pieces of software. We used our limited software budget to make sure that each first-grade teacher had the chosen program available, either from the server or on the classroom machine. When appropriate, we also provided access from computers in the school lab. Technical personnel make it their first priority to install software on the computers, and curriculum specialists show teachers techniques for using the technology in the classroom.

In the 1999–2000 school year, we identified benchmarks for technology that has the greatest impact. For instance, we have decided to introduce the practice of creating databases at the fourth-grade level because this tool supports the skills of collecting and analyzing large amounts of data needed for our required unit, Stories in Stone: Rocks, Minerals, and Fossils.

5. Plan and conduct routine maintenance

Supporting and maintaining the hardware purchased by a school system is perhaps the most neglected area in public education. Public educators do not yet understand that schools need a 24/7 (24 hours a day, 7 days a week) technical support system. If we believe it is important, for example, to run a web server that parents and students can access for posting of weekly homework assignments or school news, then it is essential that this service be working all the time. In Lexington, we do not have the technical staff to keep our web servers running consistently, so we rely mostly on a volunteer network of teachers, parents, and community experts to help out. Naturally, the quality of sites depends on the availability of volunteer help.

Lexington is fortunate to have one part-time technical support person (called a technology facilitator) in each elementary school, one full-time facilitator at each middle school, and three full-time facilitators at the high school. Their job is to keep the car running—the gas tank full, the systems in good condition—so the classroom teachers and students can easily do the driving. We also have four full-time system-wide technical staff people to keep hardware, software, and our network (including servers) running and maintained for curricular and administrative use.

Even so, we are finding that the technical staff is usually in fire-fighting mode, responding to emergencies. This year we are focusing on preventing the fires from starting by reviewing our systems that support the technical infrastructure. Our goal is to develop procedures that free up time for better planning and implementation. For example, we are developing common procedures in all schools for setting up and maintaining servers as well as installing instructional software. Standardizing the technical infrastructure wherever possible will make it easier for us to pool our resources. We will thus be able to easily deploy a team of tech facilitators to one building to accomplish a large project, such as setting up a lab or dealing with a schoolwide computer virus. Continuing to clarify the roles and responsibilities of technical staff will also help us avoid duplication of effort.

6. Provide support for curricular integration

It is not enough to have the right hardware and software available. Teachers need support to determine how to integrate the technology into the curriculum. At the elementary level, for example, we have one half-time instructional technology specialist (ITS) for three elementary schools. The ITS works directly with the classroom teachers by modeling lessons and helping to identify management strategies for using technology in the classroom.

We have begun to identify one pilot classroom per elementary grade level (called the EdLink classroom because the original funds for the first- and fifth-grade pilots came from a Bell Atlantic EdLink grant). To date, we have an EdLink first, third, and fifth grade in each school, and we plan to expand yearly until every grade level is represented. Each classroom has five computers and targeted support from the ITS. They are the first to use the technology-enhanced lessons that match their units. The EdLink teacher at a given grade level is expected to mentor and support his or her colleagues at that level. In this way, we have expanded our curricular support. A teacher may have the opportunity to work with the ITS only once a week, so whenever possible the EdLink teacher provides additional help.

Because of budget cuts in the last few years, we have not yet developed this same level of curricular support at the secondary level. We are considering alternative ways to support middle school and high school teachers, such as releasing experienced teachers—those gifted in integrating technology into the classroom—to model lessons and support their colleagues.

7. Provide ongoing training

Almost every article about using technology in the schools emphasizes the importance of adequate and ongoing training and support for using technology in the classroom. Yet most schools do not provide professional development for technology on a regular basis.

One of our real successes in Lexington was to offer extensive training for teachers in the second year of our five-year plan, during 1997–1998. We required teachers to join technology teams to learn and experiment with what we identified as core tools. These included Basic Macintosh Operations, ClarisWorks, Netscape, Eudora, and Lexington's Network. The meetings, held during teacher preparation time or when teachers were freed up for professional development, lasted one or two hours, for a total of 18 hours. Each team of 8 to 12 teachers was led by one who, as a team leader, had received specialized training.

In the third year, 1998–1999, we formed teams by grade level or department in order to examine how technology could be integrated into curriculum units or areas of study. And in 1999–2000, we offered voluntary afterschool classes and mentoring sessions by team leaders to teachers who wanted additional support. Annual reviews of core skills have shown what additional tools, training, and support are needed to meet our ever-increasing instructional needs.

Some teachers still don't see the added value of technology in the classroom. One challenge of teacher training is to make a compelling case that the technology we choose offers a *better* way of teaching and learning particular curriculum units.

8. Set up mechanisms to assess and reevaluate

A school system must develop ways to assess and evaluate progress in both the curricular and the technical areas. This year Lexington organized one elementary and one secondary task force to make recommendations about areas in which technology is essential for supporting the curriculum. What are the technology benchmarks that we want students to meet at the various grade levels? What technological skills can teachers expect students to have when they enter middle school or high school? Identifying these benchmarks will show us what we need to assess. Lexington has also hired an independent evaluator—recommended by an educational consulting firm—for two years to help us evaluate our progress and point out where we can improve. For instance, this past year, this evaluator suggested specific ways to improve our learning teams, teacher collaboration, and curriculum review.

To assess our technical and administrative support of technology, we have created two additional task forces. The organizational task force will investigate our organization for delivering technological services, and the administrative task force will evaluate our administrative systems. Using the recommendations of the four task forces, we plan to reorganize our resources and continue to fine-tune our ways of delivering both technical and instructional support for technology.

Partnerships: Making the Connection

Innovative collaborations help schools find the skills and money they need to get wired

By Karen Kelly

When it came time to connect his classrooms to the Internet, computer coordinator Don Wilder knew he was in over his head. As the director of computer instruction at the Lincoln Akerman School in Hampton Falls, NH, Wilder had spent years teaching word processing and basic programming on a collection of old computers set up in a storage closet. But by 1996, it was clear the K-8 school was overdue for a technological makeover. Since the financial and technical resources weren't readily available, the school turned to the community for help.

"During our open house, I started asking parents what fields they worked in, trying to find people who knew about computers. We also hung a big sign on the side of the building, asking for skilled volunteers," says Wilder. "Before we knew it, we had 12 to 15 people who were knowledgeable about computers and who felt it was important for the school to improve its resources."

As schools struggle to keep up with the advances in technology, administrators are increasingly turning to community and corporate volunteers for financial backing and expertise. Michael Kaufman, the founder of NetDay, a nonprofit organization that links schools with community and corporate partners, says this has changed the way schools relate to the world around them. "When a partner comes in who has a lot of resources, they can exert influence over the direction of a school," says Kaufman. "It can cause administrators to shift their priorities, or accelerate something they were planning to do all along. The school isn't an isolated place anymore."

People Power

At Lincoln Akerman, those outside influences came in the form of parents and community volunteers. The school recruited knowledgeable parents for a technology committee to create a timeline and game plan for networking classrooms. The committee aimed to connect at least one computer in each classroom to the Internet by the end of the school year. But first, they had to design a network of wiring and hardware to get the classrooms online.

Wilder says the experience that community volunteers, especially committee leaders Bob Phillips and Jim Morriss, brought to the planning was invaluable. "Without them, we would have taken shortcuts to save money that in the long run would have produced major headaches," says Wilder. "But they were people who knew what things cost. They had wired their own businesses and they knew what we needed."

With a plan in place, Wilder says the project quickly began to take shape. Local companies pitched in with donations of central networking hardware. The school's parent-teacher organization collected $2,800 to buy wiring, connectors, conduits, and outlet jackboxes. The biggest savings came in the form of labor: 40 volunteers signed up for a schoolwide technology work day. Technology committee leaders organized the volunteers into teams: unskilled workers fed wires through the ceilings into the classrooms; those with construction experience drilled holes for wires in the concrete walls; and volunteer carpenters and electricians connected the wires from the central wire panel to the outlet jacks in the classrooms.

By the end of the day, 18 classrooms, 11 offices, the library, and the computer lab were wired and Internet-ready. "It was hard to believe it could be done in a day," says Wilder. "But by having people on teams with each team knowing what they had to do, all of the jobs were done simultaneously. If we had to hire a contractor, we never would have been able to afford it."

Parents and neighbors at the Poplar Bridge Elementary School in Bloomington, MN, organized a similar grassroots effort. They figured if they could get enough volunteers to "run" wires, the school could dedicate more of its funding to individual computers. Dozens of parents, teachers, and administrators showed up for the first volunteer day in 1995. An employee of a local high-tech firm provided training for volunteers who threaded cables through walls and assembled computer stations. Even third- and fourth-grade students helped out, serving cookies and cleaning up.

Principal Gail Swor says the volunteer day built much more than a computer network. "One of the major benefits that came out of the wiring project was it brought parents and teachers together for the good of the school," says Swor. "The camaraderie was invigorating. There was excitement and laughter in the air. I don't know how I could have organized something that would have had the same result."

Now that their schools are networked, both Swor and Wilder say that such good will has continued. Parents have looked for other volunteer opportunities, such as offering tech support in the student computer labs.

Wilder believes the volunteer effort also has raised public awareness in his area of the need for technology in schools. "When our school budget went up for a vote, they placed the $17,000 we were asking for computer equipment on a separate ballot. The public voted down the budget but approved our request," says Wilder. "This project got more people invested in the school, so they understand what's involved in technology education now."

Corporate Networking

But as the majority of schools become wired to the Internet, their needs are changing. Parents and volunteers were able to help build the infrastructure. Now many schools find themselves lacking the resources to buy equipment. A growing number of educators, like Gail Swor, have had to turn to corporations for help.

"Corporate involvement has just blossomed, and I look at that as a positive thing," says Swor, who's received grants from corporations like Mobil and Asanti, a high-tech firm. "We clearly need their financial backing because our budgets haven't increased in a long time. Without it, I don't know how we would proceed."

Michael Kaufman has witnessed a similar change in his San Francisco-based organization, NetDay. It began in 1995 as a grassroots effort that recruited volunteers in California through its web site. The organization encouraged community members to organize a NetDay volunteer effort in their local schools and offered discounts on wiring kits. Almost 100,000 volunteers signed on, and with the support of the Clinton administration, the organization has spread to all 50 states and worldwide.

Kaufman's original idea linked communities and schools. But it wasn't long before he realized that high costs meant that corporate partners were needed as well. Companies like Apple, Netscape, Yahoo, and Sun Microsystems helped the organization get started by donating advertising space and thousands of wiring kits. Now NetDay matches corporations and nonprofits with schools that need technology partners. Ironically, that success can make it harder to engage communities in school technology efforts, Kaufman says. "As corporations and the government get more involved, the local people tend to move away from the project," he says. "It doesn't provide the grassroots stimulus to get them involved anymore. But we end up with more financial support. I see that as being part of our success."

However, some fear these partnerships could give corporations too much influence over a school's day-to-day activities. Kaufman agrees that an influx of funding can change an administrator's priorities. And he says it's important that educators keep in mind that every business has an agenda.

"We have great partners who've been extremely generous in the resources they've provided to schools," says Kaufman. "But it would be unreasonable to think that they don't want other schools in the district to take a look at their product being successfully implemented. They want to use those schools as a showcase later on."

Gail Swor says the companies she's worked with have had a hands-off policy, but she admits that corporate influence is something that can't be ignored. "It raises a low level of concern. Our district was so involved, the school board adopted a policy that grants must be approved by them, to make sure they're compatible with the district's mission," says Swor. "It's a smart move, since we're encouraging more of these partnerships."

In fact, Swor has already seen one offer she received turned down. After discussing it with the district's technology director, she discovered it was something the district already had in place. But she's keeping an eye out for other possibilities—all the while staying focused on what's best for students at Poplar Bridge.

"A good partnership has to have a shared vision," says Swor. "Their needs have to meet ours—and hopefully, that's to advance the use of technology throughout the curriculum."

For Further Information

Bloomington Public Schools, 8900 Portland Ave. So., Bloomington, MN 55420; tel: 612-885-8450; fax: 612-885-8640. **www.bloomington.K12.mn.us**

Lincoln Akerman School, Rt. 88 and Lafayette Rd., Hampton Falls, NH 03844; tel: 603-926-2539. **www.sau21.k12.nh.us/las**

NetDay, 15707 Rockfield Blvd., Suite 110, Irvine, CA 92618; tel: 949-609-4660; fax: 949-609-4665; e-mail: netday@netday.org. **www.netday.org**

Commentary by Karen Smith

"Each community has a wealth of technical expertise"

What are some effective ways to motivate teachers to learn and integrate new technologies into schools? HEL put this question to Karen Smith, executive director of TECH CORPS, a national nonprofit that rallies volunteers and corporations to assist K-12 schools with technology equipment and training. Her reply:

Thanks to the commitment of corporate America and local, state, and federal governments, much has been done to wire and equip our classrooms. But, successful implementation of technology in schools must be measured by its positive impact on teaching and learning, not by how much technology a school has. The new emphasis on technology training for teachers is a step in the right direction. Online courses, distance learning, professional workshops, peer-to-peer mentoring, and train-the-trainer programs are providing teachers with the knowledge they need to more effectively use technology in K-12 classrooms. But to feel confident and comfortable, teachers require something else: technical support and handholding.

Imagine the following scenario. Ms. Jones attends an all-day workshop to train on specific software that will greatly enhance her ninth-grade biology class. She is excited to incorporate what she has learned, but back in her classroom something in the software doesn't work. Although she does what she thinks is correct, nothing appears on her screen. One of two things now happens. Either Ms. Jones, needing to focus on this week's class preparation, sets the new program aside. Or she contacts her school's overworked technology coordinator, who puts Ms. Jones's request into the backlogged queue for later resolution.

Either way, Ms. Jones's enthusiasm begins to wane, as does her confidence in this new tool. And because she is not applying what she learned, she forgets some of the details she learned in the workshop. Now Ms. Jones's interest needs to be reenergized and the skills she has learned recaptured, all because of a simple technical glitch.

Now imagine the same scenario—except that when Ms. Jones calls the school technical coordinator, he or she immediately contacts a technology expert from the business community who, acting as a volunteer, helps troubleshoot the problem via phone, e-mail, or even a personal visit to Ms. Jones. With a quick and easy solution, Ms. Jones's enthusiasm and knowledge are kept intact and her confidence in this new instructional tool is enhanced because she knows that she has a "buddy" who will provide the support she needs.

Within each community lies a wealth of technical expertise, individuals who can assist teachers and technology coordinators by sharing their time and talents as school technology volunteers. Where can these people be found? Through town newspapers and local businesses, and through organizations like TECH CORPS, which rally technology volunteers to provide schools with online or in-person assistance.

How can we motivate teachers to use these new technologies in their classrooms? We can do it by providing them with the equipment and the training—*and* by providing them with a technology mentor, a knowledgeable buddy who can answer technical questions and troubleshoot problems as soon as they happen.

Equity and Technology

The Real Digital Divide: Quality Not Quantity

Closing the gap between the haves and have-nots will require much more than putting a computer in every classroom

By Maisie McAdoo

The United States has done a very good job of equipping its schools with new technology. In 1999 there was one computer for every 5.7 students, up from one per 10.8 students in 1994 and one per 19.2 in 1992. Half of U.S. classrooms are now wired for the Internet, and thanks to the "E-rate," a government-sponsored discount on the cost of wiring, all schools are due to be connected by the end of this year.

Perhaps the most striking statistic: the ratio of students to high-speed computers with Pentium processors is now virtually the same in poor schools as in affluent ones. Children in early grades take computer classes just as high school seniors do, and children of color have the same number of seats in their computer labs as do white children.

Just a few years ago, eliminating the "digital divide"—the gap between the haves and have-nots in terms of high-tech equipment—was viewed by many as education's greatest technology-related challenge. School districts formed partnerships with businesses, state and federal governments, scientific organizations, and local communities to close the gap.

And yet . . .

The equity issue persists, and in a way that is not so readily addressable by the simple installation of computers.

Necessary but Not Sufficient

The issue of equity now centers not on equality of equipment but on quality of use. The computers are there, yes, but what is the real extent of access? What kind of software is available? How much computer training are teachers getting? And are schools able to raise not just students' level of technical proficiency, but also their level of inquiry, as advanced use of technology demands?

Access to computer hardware is fairly equal, but access to interconnected computers is not. While rich and poor schools have about the same ratio of computers to kids, the poorest schools have an average of one *Internet-connected* computer per every 17 students, versus one for every ten students in wealthier districts, according to an *Education Week* special report, "Technology Counts '99."

"A lot of kids who do have access to technology in school have access to boring technology," notes Ellen Wahl of the Education Development Center's Center for Children and Technology (CCT) in New York City. Wahl says schools too often use classroom computers for fill-in-the-blanks kinds of lessons rather than projects, experiments, or construction: "The easy thing to do is drill and practice. The pedagogy makes little use of project-based learning. You have to ask, 'Did they use the Internet for research? What kinds of researchers did they become?' Being connected to the equipment is necessary but not sufficient."

Counting the computers in a school and comparing the total with other schools is straightforward; assessing what and how children are learning is another matter altogether. "We're in a developmental stage around research and evaluation in this field," Wahl explains. "The first studies were just counting hardware. Now we're getting at some aspects of use, of what kinds of experiences lead to what kinds of outcomes."

If such research is in its infancy, it is nevertheless much needed. Never before in history have so many people, unrestricted by color, gender, or income, had such ready access to vast databanks of stored knowledge. Never have so many had the means to examine, manipulate, and redefine that knowledge. The question is, Who will be taught the skills to take advantage of that wealth of information?

"What we're witnessing is the freeing up of knowledge," asserts B. Keith Fulton, director of technology programs and policy for the National Urban League. The key to maximizing the potential of new technology, Fulton believes, is well-trained teachers. "A teacher who is computer-experienced and who has training takes her students into hyper-learning mode," he says, while those without training are more likely to view the computer as a toy and surfing the Internet merely as a reward for good behavior, not an essential classroom tool.

Technological Revolution or Factory Model?

If public schools in low-income neighborhoods teach computing as a vocational programming course, they may produce a huge class of data processors, pre-trained for back-office bank jobs, while the wealthier districts train a smaller class of software engineers who can automate those office jobs out of existence. The public schools may turn out a group of Internet geeks capable of not just accessing but actually creating vast frontiers of knowledge, but, at the same time, may effectively limit access to this frontier to a techno-class, narrow and rich and white. In other words, educators may follow the paradigm of the Industrial Revolution, remaking class divisions in the old "factory model" of schooling, instead of envisioning a technological future that is enriching and democratic across class lines.

Counting the computers in a school and comparing the total with other schools is straightforward; assessing what and how children are learning is another matter altogether.

Fulton and others who are examining computer use by low-income and minority students fear that racial and class stereotypes will determine what types of applications are used in their neighborhood schools. Educators who allow the schools to mimic social norms will reinforce the pattern. "What class is the producing class, and who is at the consuming end of the digital revolution? Who gets a Web TV and a keyboard to put in the living room so they can surf as a consumer or do online gaming, and who gets computers as a tool to use, to develop software?" Fulton asks. "I don't think there's any conspiracy. It's just that people view these communities with a certain stereotype."

Caesar McDowell, an instructor at the Massachusetts Institute of Technology and Harvard Graduate School of Education, says low-income students must have opportunities to harness technology toward objectives that make sense to them as emerging artists, scientists, and community leaders. McDowell is a founder of the Civil Rights Telecommunications Forum, which looks into the civil rights implications of the 1996 Telecommunications Act. "Technology can facilitate in very powerful ways, particularly for students least served by our institutions," he says. "But there's a goal outside of the technology which we are trying to reinforce, rather than 'We've got to have the technology.'"

How Inequities Persist

If we revisit the access question from the perspective of quality of use rather than quantity of computers, inequities rapidly become apparent.

Middle-class schools are more likely to have full-time, school-based technology coordinators. While this valuable resource is scarce enough in richer schools, it is actually declining in poor ones. *Education Week* found that 30 percent of U.S. schools had full-time technology coordinators in 1998, up one percentage point from 1996. But in schools where more than 70 percent of students qualified for free lunch, only 19 percent had full-time coordinators in 1998, down from 26 percent two years before.

Wealthier schools also supplement district-funded hardware with additional technology, such as video production labs, scientific labs with computer-connected probes and sensors, and CAD/CAM design programs. They may have parent volunteers who work in the software industry. Their administrators are more likely to know how to bring in corporate interest and sponsorship.

These extras make the difference between minimally sufficient computer training and outstanding programs. These are the same sorts of disparities that poor children encounter in all their other subjects and outside of school as well. The inequality is not in the equipment tally but in access to extra resources. In this way schools are failing in their mission as equalizers, and more of the burden falls on families and communities to ensure that their children learn about technology.

Computer Access Outside of School

To master technology, children need not just a two-week computer class but fairly continuous access throughout their education. As in any apprenticeship, the learning curve for technology is long and has several stages. It requires mentoring and guidance from someone who is already accomplished, plentiful access, and time to just fool around with the equipment. Students who have only an outdated computer at home, or who must wait in line at the public library to use the computer, will not easily become fluent.

Yet the digital divide is far wider in students' homes than it is in schools. According to the U.S. Commerce Department's July 1999 report, *Falling Through the Net: Defining the Digital Divide*, only about 20 percent of households with incomes below $30,000 own computers, as opposed to 80 percent of those with incomes over $75,000. Roughly 16 percent of households in which the parents did not finish high school have computers at home, versus 69 percent of those in which parents have bachelor's degrees or higher. By contrast, there is a difference of less than ten percentage points in telephone ownership between the least educated and the most educated.

What's worse, the trend is toward greater disparity. The Commerce Department reports that between 1997 and 1998, the gap in computer ownership increased by 25 percent between those at the highest and lowest educational levels and by 29 percent between those at the highest and lowest income levels.

"While we are encouraged by the dramatic growth in the access Americans have to the nation's information technologies," writes Secretary of Commerce William Daly in the introduction to *Falling Through the Net*, "the growing disparity in access between certain groups and regions is alarming." The groups most likely to be stranded on the wrong side of the divide include "certain minorities, low-income groups, and residents in rural areas and central cities."

Community-Based Initiatives: Still a Way to Go

Such disparities have not been lost on youth-serving organizations that are mounting efforts to develop afterschool technology centers and programs. These include libraries, Girls and Boys Clubs, ASPIRA, YM/YWCAs, Boy and Girl Scouts, local churches, and housing project recreation centers.

Some model programs, such as Oakland, CA's, Plugged In, the Educational Video Center in New York, and Street Level Youth Media in Chicago, involve teenagers in sophisticated computer-based documentary projects, take an analytic view of media and information, and give students open-ended learning opportunities.

However, such programs require huge amounts of staff development and a high ratio of adults to kids. "The easy thing to do in these after-schools is drill and practice, write letters to the Spice Girls, things like that," says CCT's Wahl. Generally, the quality of programs in afterschool centers has been poor.

Yolanda George, deputy director for education at the American Association for the Advancement of Science, laments that most afterschool programs have focused just on getting the computers. Because they are drop-in centers, they may have inconsistent training and little professional development for staff. George explains: "There's a rush to set up all this technology, but the same type of attention isn't paid to the quality of what's going on in these centers. No one's really thought beyond what happens once you've gotten the center set up."

George and Wahl, with others, have just completed a study of out-of-school technology programs. They found a "huge range" in the quality of programs and little systematic effort to improve them. "Many of the youth organizations are just beginning to figure out what good programs look like," says George.

The researchers examined what agendas the programs had for the children they served, what types of math and science activities they offered, and what was needed to strengthen the effort. Many of the programs, George notes, are taught by moonlighting public school teachers or part-time college students who don't bring any special expertise to the centers, and few are related to school curricula. But, she adds, "you still have to have educational standards in the out-of-school setting."

In spite of their shortcomings, the researchers conclude, the informal community centers do help compensate for deficits in the schools and give students opportunities for less-structured access to computers.

Structuring Schools for Technology

Most children take to computers like fish to water. As one Florida computer teacher observes: "It's always been that you find children who are better at things than their teachers. In technology, almost all kids are better than almost all teachers."

Perhaps technology is a generational badge; perhaps it's just fun. "What computers add is an element of excitement and motivation. It's hands-on, it's something you own," says the Urban League's Fulton. "It leads to collateral resources, people working together, communicating overseas. It teaches children how the real world works."

Often, what holds students back is not the technology but the structure of schools. Traditional or fearful teachers may not tolerate the kinds of exploratory, "nonlinear," constructivist approaches that students bring to web surfing and computer use. A student who is expert in the technology can be a threat to a math or science teacher. Or the school day may be organized so that access to computers is limited or time is not set aside to work on small-group or individual projects.

The question for educators is what kinds of schools will build every student's technological skills. In part, students need lots of time online to build familiarity with computers. In part, they need good computer teachers. And they need non-computer skills—the ability to synthesize information, ask further questions, compare, contrast, write, and evaluate.

Equity is achieved not just when whites and blacks, rich and poor students master an equal number of software applications, but when all students use their minds well. "The equity issue," as Wahl puts it, "is way beyond hardware and even beyond connectivity and probably related to offline skills like literacy."

The Work Force in the New Millennium

The students who graduate from high school in 2000 and beyond will have to find their way in a fast-changing workplace environment. Coping and communication skills, entrepreneurial skills like identifying markets and designing and developing products, and problem-solving and management skills will be more and more prized, while the simple ability to show up for work and do what you're told will lose value.

"It is important that kids have basic computer skills, but they're not the bottleneck," asserts Richard Murnane of the Harvard Graduate School of Education. "The bottleneck is being able to think carefully and creatively and having interactive skills. The increase in computers in work forces is reducing the demand for human beings to do routine information processing and raising the demand for distinctly human skills such as communication, teamwork, and model-based problem-solving."

In fact, today's recent college graduates, who live by the Internet and are masters of computing, are part of a new work culture that may turn out to be as revolutionary in its way as the Industrial Revolution was 200 years ago. The efficiencies created by computers mean sharp drops in industrial employment and a surge in jobs that require thinking. Employment is more transitory and guarantees are fewer. People are far more internationalist, since they speak as easily to Jakarta as to New Jersey. Social changes may be even more radical as young people create their own nomadic culture, one not subject to corporate loyalty.

In this culture, equity will result both from computer skills and from young people's ability to apply those skills in new ways. From this perspective, the issue of technological equity becomes a broader issue of educational equity, at once tougher but more familiar, requiring whole-school reform, and demanding to be solved.

For Further Information

Center for Children and Technology, 96 Morton St., New York, NY 10014; tel: 212-807-4200; fax: 212-633-8804; e-mail: cct@edc.org. **www2.edc.org/CCT/cctweb**

Civil Rights Forum on Communications Policy (formerly the Civil Rights Telecommunications Forum), 818 18th St., N.W., Suite 505, Washington, DC 20006; tel: 202-887-0301; fax: 202-887-0305; e-mail: forum@civilrightsforum.org. **www.civilrightsforum. org**

Closing the Digital Divide. A web site of the U.S. Department of Commerce. **www. digitaldivide.gov**

The Digital Divide Network. A web site sponsored by the Benton Foundation. **www. digitaldividenetwork.org**

Educational Video Center, 55 E. 25th St., Suite 407, New York, NY 10010; tel: 212-725-3534; fax: 212-725-6501. **www.cpprev.org/educavideo.htm**

National Telecommunications and Information Administration. *Falling Through the Net III: Defining the Digital Divide.* Washington, DC: U.S. Department of Commerce, July 1999. **www.ntia.doc.gov/ntiahome/fttn99/contents.html**

B. Keith Fulton, Director of Technology Programs and Policy, The National Urban League, 120 Wall St., New York, NY 10005. **www.nul.org**

Yolanda George, Deputy Director for Education, American Association for the Advancement of Science, 1200 New York Ave., N.W., Washington, DC 20005; tel: 202-326-6400. **www.aaas.org**

Losing Ground Bit by Bit: Low-Income Communities in the Information Age (1998). The Benton Foundation, 950 18th St., N.W., Washington, DC 20006; tel: 202-638-5770; toll free: 877-223-6866; fax: 202-638-5771; e-mail: benton@benton.org. **www.benton. org**

Caesar McDowell, Associate Professor of the Practice of Community Development, Department of Urban Studies and Planning. Massachusetts Institute of Technology, 77 Massachusetts Ave., Cambridge, MA 02139.

R. Murnane and F. Levy. *Teaching the New Basic Skills: Principles for Educating Children to Thrive in a Changing Economy.* New York: Free Press, 1996.

Plugged In, 1923 University Ave., E. Palo Alto, CA 94303; tel 650-322-1134; fax: 650-322-6147; e-mail: info@pluggedin.org. **www.pluggedin.org**

Street-Level Youth Media, 1856 W. Chicago Ave., 1st Floor, Chicago, IL 60622; tel: 773-862-5331; fax: 773-862-0754; e-mail: admin@street-level.org. **http://streetlevel.iit.edu**

"Technology Counts '99: Building the Digital Curriculum." A collaboration of *Education Week* and the Milken Exchange. Education Week, 6935 Arlington Rd., Suite 100, Bethesda, MD 20814-5233; tel: 301-280-3100; fax: 301-280-3250. **www.edweek.org**

Commentary by Milton Chen

"Internet content should reflect children's diversity of needs and interests"

What can be done to bridge the digital divide in education? HEL asked Milton Chen, executive director of the George Lucas Educational Foundation, to reply:

Fundamentally, technology cannot be used effectively or even ethically unless it is distributed and used equitably among all groups in our society and our increasingly smaller world. While the digital divide has become part of our national agenda, there are still teachers, as master teacher Bonnie Bracey has noted, who do not have a POT (plain old telephone) in their classrooms! If computer technology is to have widespread impact on learning, communication, and community, it cannot be limited to those with greater educational and financial resources.

Just as equality of educational opportunity is central to our nation's democracy, "equality of digital opportunity" is fast becoming its synonym. In fact, inequities in access to computer technology may ultimately prove illegal. Consider the implications if, in 2004, on the 50th anniversary of the landmark *Brown v. Board of Education* decision on school desegregation, a group of parents sues their school board for denying their children's right of access to computers and the resources of the Internet.

To provide greater equality of digital opportunity, a broader definition of equity is needed. Equity should not be measured in terms of number of computers alone. More refined measures should include the quality of computers, child-to-computer ratios, and the speed of Internet connectivity. Children with access to T-1 lines and CD-ROM players have a great advantage over those with 28K modems and floppy disks.

This broader definition should go even further, beyond the "boxes and wires," to include psychological dimensions of attitudes and interests. Consider two teens who live in the same neighborhood, go to the same school, and have similar family backgrounds and socioeconomic status. One of them uses the community technology center to design web sites for local businesses. Another has never stepped in the door. What accounts for the difference? One of public education's roles is to light a fire within children so they see technology as an important and enjoyable way of learning and communicating. Equity requires that we offer appealing content and compelling role models to encourage greater numbers of young people to cross the digital divide.

Community technology centers (CTCs) in low-income neighborhoods offer one of the most promising solutions. The U.S. Department of Education has provided $20 million to CTCs in public libraries, community organizations, and public housing facilities. New findings on Internet use by low-income users by the Children's Partnership suggest that CTCs can encourage a communal style of computer use, where children and adults share their experiences and support each other within a community setting. If computers and the Internet can bring people together and create new kinds of community arrangements, both in person and through virtual groups, the implications can be profound, merging "high tech" with "high touch."

Internet content should also reflect the diversity of children's needs and interests across age groups, gender, geography, and languages. Here, the computer's parallels to television are instructive. TV has not fulfilled its original promise of being a window on the world for children in part because of the scarce availability of educational content. In order for new forms of "digital TV" and web content to fulfill their potential, high-quality content remains key. Already some excellent examples of educational content can be found, as mentioned elsewhere in this book. And just as educational TV developed new formats and techniques for creatively delivering educational content, digital media can build upon the best in older media of children's books, games, and TV, as well as earlier software, to design new forms of digital content.

Bridging the digital divide also requires models of change—success stories—that shatter stereotypes and inspire action. The media's role is vital in spreading these stories. At the George Lucas Educational Foundation, we are developing a multimedia project on teachers and technology, to be distributed via the Web, books, and cassettes. We are also publishing a newsletter chronicling exemplary teachers and students using technology in underserved schools and communities. Impressive stories of Internet use by senior citizens, inner-city youth, recent immigrants, and family farmers show others how technology can benefit everyone. In the national effort to cross the digital divide, today's pathfinders are charting a road map for many others to follow.

This article is adapted from a longer piece that will appear in The Future of Children: Children and Computer Technology, *which will be published by The David and Lucille Packard Foundation later this year (**www.futureofchildren. org**)*.

The Gender Gap: Why Do Girls Get Turned Off to Technology?

As more boys than girls grow up wanting careers in technology, schools and researchers try to make computers more appealing to girls

By Karen Kelly

Teacher Connie Dow got tired of watching the boys in her fifth-grade classroom monopolize the computer. They were always there—playing games, trying new programs, surfing the Web. The girls, meanwhile, seemed hesitant to use the computer and gravitated to other activities instead. That bothered Dow. In this class of gifted students at the Central Accelerated School in Chillicote, MO, she expected girls to assert themselves in all areas. So Dow started a weeklong summer camp where girls could learn computer technology without having to compete with boys.

At camp, the girls learned not only how to use computers more effectively but also how to build and maintain them. "By the end of the week, they could also clean the computers, install software, access the Internet, and serve as the school's webmaster," Dow says. With fresh knowledge of motherboards and C drives, the girls became part of the school's tech support team, coaching other students and teachers in how to troubleshoot problems. They even dismantled and cleaned the principal's computer. "When you're a fifth grader, working on the principal's computer is a big deal," says Dow. "You can hear the confidence in their voices, and their parents and teachers see them differently now. The expectations are higher for the girls because they have these skills."

There is widespread concern among educators and parents that girls are being left behind in computer science. Not only do girls report being less interested in computers than boys, but by the time they graduate from high school, far fewer of them pursue careers in computer science.

"This isn't a case of mass phobia," says Pamela Haag, director of research at the American Association of University Women (AAUW). "But software, teaching methods, even the course descriptions don't resonate with them. And we're losing talent as a result." In response, many schools are starting special programs, such as clubs and summer camps, in order to spark girls' interest in technology.

Few Differences in Computer Use

Are girls in fact less techno-friendly, or is that just the perception? Judging by available statistics, it can be hard to tell. A recent Kaiser Family Foundation Report, "Kids and Media at the New Millenium," found that among children eight and older, girls and boys spend about the same amount of time per day on computers—32 minutes for girls and 38 minutes for boys. UCLA researchers found similar statistics on computer usage among college freshmen, where 68 percent of male students used e-mail in 1998, compared to 64.2 percent of females. About the same disparity separated those using the Internet for research.

There is also little evidence of a gap in achievement in technical subjects. Studies from the Department of Education's National Center for Education Statistics (NCES) show high school girls are taking the same higher-level math and science classes as the boys, and performing almost as well. On the National Assessment of Educational Progress (NAEP), 63 percent of 17-year-old boys performed well on upper-level math questions, compared to 58 percent of the girls. In the general science assessment, 83.8 percent of boys did well, compared to 83.7 percent of the girls. "There's been a lot of talk about the gender divide, but it appears it's not very large," says Tom Snyder, a researcher with NCES. "However, when it's time to go to college, something changes. Something happens in the pipeline."

One of the first indicators of this gender disparity may be the Advanced Placement exam in computer science. Girls accounted for only 17 percent of the test-takers on the A exam and 9 percent on the more difficult AB exam. In 1996, almost three times as many men earned bachelor's degrees in computer science as did women. And the more challenging the computer science degree, the smaller the percentage of women who pursued it. That disparity "has a real impact on future earnings," says Snyder.

Ironically, the gender gap is closing in other scientific fields. According to the 1998 *Digest of Education Statistics*, published by NCES, "other technical fields have been driven upward in recent years, in part by increasing numbers of female graduates." The report found the number of biological science degrees awarded to women increased 60 percent between 1991 and 1996. They now earn more biology degrees than men. In the physical sciences, 37 percent more women earned a bachelor's in 1996 than five years earlier. And in the fields of agriculture and natural resources, the number of female graduates grew by 84 percent over the five-year period. While male graduates still outnumber females in the physical sciences and natural resources, women are clearly showing more interest in these scientific fields.

"Girls see these sciences as areas with lots of teamwork and social interaction," says Maria Klawe, dean of science at the University of British Columbia (UBC). "But they visualize computer scientists as nerds." Klawe, herself a computer scientist, has spent the past seven years trying to figure out why girls lose interest in computer science. Her study of 7,300 girls in grades 8, 10, and 12 came up with familiar findings—that girls use computers for their schoolwork and e-mail at about the same rate as boys. But their perceptions about computer science get more negative as the girls get older, Klawe found. "Girls are turned off to computer science as early as grade 8. They think they're no good at it," says Klawe, who teaches information sciences. "By the time they reach grade 12, it's even worse. And since girls rate personal interest and personal ability as the top reasons for choosing a career, very few of them pursue computer science."

What Role Do Video Games Play?

The question is why. One answer may be found in a growing piece of pop culture: video games. "Games are an entry point into the computer world," says UCLA education professor Yasmin Kafai. "No matter what they teach you, computer games give you a familiarity with technology. And that gives you a leg up. When I worked with first and second graders, you could tell right away which ones played games."

More often than not, those students are boys. On a typical day, 55 percent of boys aged eight to 18 play computer games every day versus

23 percent of girls, according to the Kaiser Family Foundation study. Boys also play longer—30 minutes a day compared to only eight minutes for girls. And 17 percent of boys reported spending more than an hour a day on games, as opposed to just 4 percent of the girls.

The problem, according to Kafai, is that girls aren't interested in most of the computer games out there. She realized this when she asked fourth and fifth graders to design games that would test the player's knowledge of fractions. "All of the boys' created games that incorporated violent feedback. If you got an answer wrong, you'd be transformed into an ice cube or sent frying into the underworld," says Kafai, author of *Minds in Play: Computer Game Design as a Context for Children's Learning.* "None of the girls' games had that. And rather than using fantasy, as the boys did, the girls drew on real-life situations to design the game. They didn't emulate what was already out there in video games." Rather, girls wanted games that required strategy and skill, but that had life-like characters they could relate to.

Klawe of UBC notices another difference. She designs games to test math skills and then observes how boys and girls use them. "The boys move much faster through games and activities. So they will do better in anything that measures progress by the number of problems solved," says Klawe. "The girls, on the other hand, are less interested in how far they progress and more interested in the experience of the game. They like to explore more in-depth. And when we have measured what they learned, the girls have done just as well as the boys."

But that approach is not found in most computer games on the market, says AAUW's Pamela Haag. The result is that boys get interested in games and the technology, stay interested, and eventually pursue careers in an industry that will continue to interest and attract youngsters just like themselves. "We often say girls have to catch up with technology, but I think computer technology has to catch up with girls. Teachers and game designers need to use more meaningful problem sets and examples and they have to show how it relates to real problems. We need more women designing these games," says Haag.

Of course, there's the chicken-and-egg riddle. If fewer women are going into technology careers, how can we expect to see more games oriented toward girls? Says Haag: "Because games don't appeal to girls, they aren't getting that playful exposure to computer technology that would quicken their interest in learning more about it."

Single-Sex Solution?

Games are just one part of the puzzle solution. Klawe's work with classroom teachers in the Vancouver area confirms what Connie Dow found in Missouri: that single-sex computer sessions help girls. "The boys just grab the computers, while the girls are much more hesitant to take ownership, even when it's their fair turn," says Klawe. "When we established separate computer times for boys and girls, the girls were much more enthusiastic. It made them feel like they were supposed to be there." Klawe also had better results with single-sex feedback sessions when she talked to students about their computer use. "When the boys and girls were together," she says, "the boys participated more. But alone, the girls had just as much to say."

In fact, single-sex solutions to the technology gender gap are becoming increasingly popular, both in and out of the classroom. Afterschool clubs, technology career fairs, and mentoring programs are providing girls with new opportunities.

Kathleen Bennett took that idea one step further when, in 1998, she founded the technology-centered Girls' Middle School in Mountain View, CA. "For me, it's kind of a no-brainer. The research shows when you have an all-girls environment, there's no one to cast a shadow over what girls are doing," says Bennett. Math, science, and technology take center stage at the private school. Since students attend for only three years (grades 6-8), Bennett says she wants to make sure she offers them something unique. "We thought about what they'll be learning elsewhere and decided to put more emphasis on subjects like computer science, engineering, and the physical sciences, because we know girls don't do as well in those subjects," says Bennett, who included an engineer and a software developer on her staff. "In the programming class, they're learning how to create web pages in HTML and use Stagecast Creator [a programming tool that creates games]. Our goal is to have them programming in Java by the end of eighth grade."

Of course, the single-sex approach does have its critics, especially in publicly funded schools where boys are excluded from certain special programs. Diane Ravitch, a fellow at the Manhattan Institute and a former assistant secretary of education under George Bush, disagrees that girls and boys have different learning styles with regard to technology—or any other subject. "It gets to be incredibly sexist when we say here's what you can do in the kitchen, so this must be the way you learn. I don't think we should have sexist approaches to teaching technology or anything else."

The AAUW has come under fire from some for advocating girls-only camps and clubs. "If these programs are funded by tax dollars, they can't discriminate by gender," says University of Alaska gender specialist Judith Kleinfeld. "Boys, especially minority boys, also need computer skills. I would like to see mixed-gender technology programs that offer a range of gender groupings and learning materials. Flexible groupings within a classroom offers the advantages of single-sex classrooms without the unfairness."

But the AAUW's Haag argues that the single-sex solution to the technology gap could serve as useful model for addressing the digital divide among other groups as well: "A lot of these suggestions apply to other groups that aren't flocking into the information technology profession—like African American boys and Hispanics. The people not taking these classes have good reasons for not taking them. We need to make them more interesting for everyone."

In a sense, both parties are right, says Marcia Linn, professor at the University of California, Berkeley. Technology needs to be taught in a way that is relevant to all students—male or female—and that engages them in problem-based learning. "There's no one size fits all," says Linn, co-author of *Computers, Teachers, Peers: Science Learning Partners*. "Students are really diverse, and certain arrangements, like single-sex education, will be better for some than for others. The most important aspect of equity is to have effective teaching that motivates the students. When we improve instruction, boys and girls learn very similarly."

Finding Good Games for Girls

Video games have been blamed for everything from inciting violence to decaying children's minds. But while there's concern about their content, growing evidence suggests that those who play computer games—mostly boys—have an advantage in pursuing careers in computer science. This has led researchers like Maria Klawe at the University of British Columbia to draw attention to the girl-friendly games that are on the market. "I tell parents to think about what their daughter is interested in and then find a computer activity that will foster that," says Klawe. Some games are specifically designed for girls. Characters like Barbie, Nancy Drew, Buffy the Vampire Slayer, and Madeline all have their own software programs. Klawe says some of these games are more valuable than others. She asked her college students to review many of them for a web site maintained by the Supporting Women in Information Technology (SWIFT) program, which she founded (see **taz.cs.ubc. ca/swift/fun/gamereview.html**).

Another web site that offers reviews of video game software is called Through the Glass Wall: Computer Games for Mathematical Empowerment (**www.terc.edu/mathequity/gw/html/gwhome. html**). The site was created by TERC, a research organization focused on improving math and science education, to assess both the educational and entertainment value of computer games. The site also offers a bibliography of books and articles on the topic. TERC researchers have also recognized the need to engage girls with computer games. Its web site reads: "While computer games could provide the opportunity for increased mathematical learning by both boys and girls, the reality is that girls are not benefiting from the potential of computers to promote math learning. For girls, the computer's screen seems to be a kind of glass wall." A wall that perhaps some fun and games can help tear down.

For Further Information

American Association of University Women, 1111 16th St. N.W., Washington, DC 20036; tel: 800-326-AAUW; fax: 202-872-1425; e-mail: info@aauw.org.

The Girls' Middle School, 180 North Rengstorff Ave., Mountain View, CA 94043; tel: 650-968-8338; fax: 650-968-4775; e-mail: gms@girlsms.org. **www.girlsms.org**

J. Kleinfeld. *The Myth That Schools Shortchange Girls.* Washington, DC: Women's Freedom Network, 1998.

Y.B. Kafai. *Minds in Play: Computer Game Design as a Context for Children's Learning.* Rahway, NJ: Erlbaum, 1995.

M.C. Linn and S. Hsi. *Computers, Teachers, Peers: Science Learning Partners.* Rahway, NJ: Erlbaum, 2000.

A Title IX for the Technology Divide?

Can our efforts to close the gender gap in sports teach us how to resolve inequities in access to technology, too?

By Margaret Riel

P roblems of inequity often seem hopeless, as if they are part of the fabric of life that cannot be altered. The current growing digital divide compounds the effects of racial, economic, and gender inequities. Yet there are numerous examples throughout history of how courageous actions, petitions, programs, and laws have altered the balance of power and increased equity of opportunities. To stimulate our thinking about solutions to the digital divide, I'd like to draw a parallel to past gender inequity in sports and the role that a particular programmatic intervention played in altering some of the dimensions of the problem. But first, it is important to understand the dimensions of the digital divide because it is multi-dimensional, extends well beyond the school, and affects different groups of people.

The digital divide has physical dimensions.

Poor, minority, or female students are less likely to have access to the computers at school or at home. In the 1998 Teaching, Learning, and Computing (TLC) Survey, Henry Becker and Ronald Anderson found that the ratio of students to computers has decreased for all schools to an average of seven students to each school computer. Minority schools have fewer computers, but the differences are not as dramatic as they have been in the past. The existence of a digital divide appears in student access to multimedia computers necessary for working with the Internet. They found a ratio of 70 students to one multimedia computer in high-minority schools, compared to 25 to one in schools with few or no minority students. The National Telecommunications and Information Administration report, *Falling Through the Net: Defining the Digital Divide*, shows that students from white families are nearly twice as likely to have a computer at home than students from African American or Hispanic families. And, according to the 1998 Roper Youth Survey, boys were more likely than girls to have their own computer (17 percent to 10 percent, although girls were as likely to use computers in the home).

The digital divide has communication dimensions.

Students in low socioeconomic areas are less likely to have connections to the Internet at school or at home. The responses of 4,000 teachers from the TLC survey indicate that in spring of 1998, 90 percent of U.S. schools were connected to the Internet. However, the schools in the richest communities are more than twice as likely to have very high-speed lines as those in the poorest communities.

Falling Through the Net shows that a similar pattern exists in the home, where households with incomes of $75,000 and higher are more than *20 times* more likely to have access to the Internet than those at the lowest income levels. In addition, white students are three times more likely to have Internet connections than students from either African American or Hispanic families. While there does not appear to be as much of a gender gap in home Internet access, girls appear to use the connection in different ways. The 1998 Roper Youth Study found that girls were more likely to use the Internet for communication and the boys were more likely to play games and download software.

The digital divide has conceptual/skill dimensions.

Teachers shape the use of computers in schools. The TLC data indicates that teachers who received higher grades from better universities and who continue their professional development were more likely to value the use of computer technology in schools and have students use it to analyze and present information. Teachers who teach in low socioeconomic communities had less education and were substantially more likely to use computers to remediate skills. School districts often find it easier to acquire computers than to help teachers learn how to use them to design effective learning environments. Without teachers who understand technology, students from minority schools and female students are not learning how to control the technology and remain underrepresented in advanced computer courses.

In 1996, 83 percent of the students who took the AP test in computer science were male. The percentage of women in information technology careers has shrunk from 35 percent in the early 1990s to 29 percent in 1998, according to the U.S. Department of Labor. The Department of Education reports a similar decline in bachelor's degrees in computer science for women. These figures suggest that the conceptual dimension of the digital divide is increasing.

The digital divide has personal/value dimensions.

Teachers and students in low-income schools whose primary use of computers is to remediate skills are often very skeptical about the value of digital technologies. When they look across the digital divide they can see only the rocky edge, and not the possibilities that lie in more fertile valleys. In a recent television broadcast on the digital divide, teachers who work with minority students spoke passionately about the students' need to interact with each other, to understand the real world, and to attend to the important goals of education. But unlike their counterparts in more privileged schools, they lacked a clear view of how digital technologies could be used to accomplish these goals. Some teachers and students are caught in a cycle of negative attitudes toward technology that keep them from the experiences that are necessary to change the attitude.

Good teachers design their courses to build on students' prior knowledge and interests. In computer courses, where boys with years of home use of technology dominate the class, coursework decisions are made to attract their interest. The effect is a digital culture that can feel hostile to those who do not have extensive computer experience. The "problem" develops later when the consequence of minimal experience with technology leads to increased inequities in the workplace.

These four dimensions of the digital divide are listed from those that are easiest to solve to those that pose the most difficult challenges. Simplistic solutions to systemic problems can make the divide wider. For example, to solve inequities in access, some have proposed that government funds be used to provide all schools with high-speed Internet access. Schools that have multimedia computers, teachers and students who know how to use these tools, and a culture that values partnerships would benefit immediately. In poorer schools without technology and training, this universal "equal" access will carry far less value. Ironically, this simplistic technical solution, implemented in isolation, would serve to increase the digital divide.

The current government-sponsored E-rate discounts on Internet services are helping schools in low-income communities connect to the Internet. However, these gains are unlikely to have a lasting effect unless teachers have time, resources, and the motivation to learn how to teach with new technologies. Unfortunately, schools in low-income communities have fewer resources than wealthy communities for teacher education and technology support. And while teachers in wealthy schools can often depend on technically savvy students for technical support, both teachers and students in urban schools face a relatively steep learning curve without the aid of local experts.

Of course, the greatest challenge in closing the digital divide has to do with attitudes and values interacting with issues of access. In this regard, it might be instructive to examine the case of Title IX and the role it played in closing the gender gap in sports.

In 1971, only one out of 27 high school girls participated in organized sports programs, and most girls showed little interest in sports. Their athletic options focused on leading the cheers for the football or basketball game. Title IX legislation required that female students be provided an equitable opportunity to participate in sports. Schools receiving federal support were required to provide equal treatment in the provision of equipment, supplies, team scheduling, travel opportunities, coaching, practice and competitive facilities, medical services, publicity and promotions, recruitment, support services, and scholarships. As a result, there has been an explosion in the number of athletic opportunities open to women and girls of all ages and levels of ability.

More Challenges, More Success

The law was based on the assumption that boys and girls have equal interest in sports at early ages and the imbalance resulted from a lack of resources and recognition for girls' sports. Because of Title IX, more girls—one out of three in fact—are enjoying the challenges, physical training, and team spirit that come from playing organized sports. When girls wear letterman jackets today, they have their own names on them.

As a result of equal opportunities for recognition and resources in sports, the culture of growing up female in America has been significantly altered.

We know there is little or no gender difference in the computer use of very young children. While computers remain gender neutral, software programs are designed to appeal to boys. What if we created a Title IX for technology, requiring schools to demonstrate that the digital resources in their schools were being used as much by females as by males and proportionally by students from different backgrounds? In order to comply, a school would have to offer a range of courses that had the net effect of a balanced use of digital equipment by all groups of students.

Title IX did not result in female football teams, but it did produce a range of athletic programs in track, soccer, tennis, swimming, and basketball that would not exist without equal funding. If schools had to show that money spent on digital technology was equally benefiting all groups of students, how would the culture of computer use in schools change? There would be changes in the way computer classes are organized. Digital technology might find its way into art and English classes. There might be more courses that use technology to design spaces, create simulations, or express artistic designs in multimedia environments. Recent research by Kimberly Burge indicates that female students are attracted to multimedia constructive uses of technology. Perhaps a programming course in the design of interactive reading materials for young students would attract a different balance of gender. Using the computers for international collaboration is another way to draw those with less experience into the computer labs. These courses could provide the bridge of experience necessary for taking more advanced courses in computer science.

Such changes would help break down the digital divide in the commercial marketplace. Software development is dominated by male programmers who use their personal experience to generate ideas for new programs. Recent efforts to develop software for girls have resulted in programs such as one to design clothes for Barbie. Who bought this software? Anxious parents who worried that their daughters were not "playing" with the tools of societal power.

This solution insults girls' skills and knowledge. Aesthetic interests in the arts do not have to be clothed in the sexism of Barbie. We need a diverse cross section of our population to help make wise decisions as we face the many ethical and moral crossroads of online community building. We need all students to develop basic literacy with digital tools. Title IX also required an increase in funding for girls' coaches, which has been critical to turning around the gender imbalance in school sports. We desperately need funding to help teachers learn how to use computers in ways that engage girls as well as boys, students who have computer skills and those who are beginning to acquire them. Schools could take a leadership role in changing the projected image of a computer user in a way similar to how they have changed the image of who is capable of being an athlete.

Those that have power rarely give it up willingly. Many male coaches and athletes resent women's sports. However, the consequence of making room for women in sports is that now young girls look up to the women who earned the 1999 World Cup in soccer. This provides a different kid of role model than the one projected by Barbie dolls.

Increasing the range of opportunities for computer use in schools may help those who question the value of technology to see beyond computers as self-paced tutorials. The more varied the group currently using digital tools in schools, the more likely that the next generation of teachers and software designers will be able to use their personal experiences to design learning environments that attract diverse students. We need a digital world that reflects the values and cultures of a diverse population. We need clarity of vision to see the value on both sides of the digital divide.

For Further Information

Gender Gaps: Where Schools Still Fail Our Children. The American Association of University Women Educational Foundation Research, Dept. RR.INT, 1111 16th St. N.W., Washington, DC 20036; tel: 202-728-7602; e-mail: foundation@aauw.org. www.aauw.org/2000/gg.html

J. Becker. "Who's Wired and Who's Not." In *Children and Computers* (in press), The Center on the Future of Children, David and Lucille Packard Foundation, 300 Second St., Suite 200, Los Altos, CA 94022; fax: 650-948-6498. www.futureofchildren.org

K. Burge. *Multimedia Computer Learning: An Examination of Gender Difference in Computer Learning Behaviors at the Elementary Grade Level.* University of California Dissertation, UMI number 9932086, 1999.

R.J. Coley, J. Cradler, and P.K. Engel. *Computers and Classrooms: The Status of Technology in U.S. Schools.* Princeton, NJ: ETS Policy Information Center, 1997. www.ets.org/research/pic/compclass.html

T. Novak and D. Hoffman. "Bridging the Digital Divide: The Impact of Race on Computer Access and Internet Use, Project 2000." Paper presented at Vanderbilt University, Feb. 2, 1998. **www2000.ogsm.vanderbilt.edu/papers/race/science.html**

Digital Divide. TV program by Public Broadcasting Service, January 28, 2000. **www.pbs. org/digitaldivide**

Falling Through the Net III: Defining the Digital Divide. Washington, DC: U.S. Department of Commerce, National Telecommunications and Information Administration, July 1999. **www.ntia.doc.gov/ntiahome/digitaldivide**

Roper 1998 Youth Report. Available online at: **www.roper.com/news**

Teaching, Learning and Computing. Center for Research on Information Technology and Organizations, University of California at Irvine, 3200 Berkeley Pl., Irvine, CA 92697; tel: 949-824-6387; fax: 949-824-8091; e-mail: tlc@uci.edu. **www.crito.uci.edu/ TLC**

Looking Ahead

A New Century Demands New Ways of Learning

Both students and teachers need to master skills that weren't necessary in the last century but are vital in the new one

By Chris Dede

Just as advances in computing and telecommunications have improved medicine, finance, manufacturing, and numerous other sectors of society, these changes are reshaping education—transforming what we learn, how we acquire knowledge, and how our schools function. Emerging interactive media are aiding the development of richer curricula, better teaching strategies, more effective organizational structures, stronger links between schools and society, and the empowerment of disenfranchised learners. Researchers and educators who foster the dissemination of best practices are creating virtual communities of practice to empower reform in schooling. Furthermore, new interactive media promise to give all students and teachers the opportunity to learn complex concepts and skills.

As sophisticated technology alters the nature of work and citizenship, the skills and concepts students need to be productive adults are changing too. Simply aiming for higher standards of achievement in today's curriculum will not prepare pupils for 21st-century life. Students—and teachers—need to master new skills that the current curriculum may not address, skills that were not central in the industrial society of the past century but are vital in the knowledge-based economy of the new one. These skills include: the ability to collaborate with diverse teams of people—face-to-face or at a distance—to accomplish a task; to create, share, and master knowledge by assessing and filtering quasi-accurate information; and to "thrive on chaos," that is, to make rapid decisions based on that incomplete information to resolve to novel dilemmas. New technologies can help students and teachers acquire these vital skills and knowledge.

Of course, new learning technologies are only worth the time, effort, and resources required for widespread implementation when they are used appropriately. Technology is not a "vitamin" whose mere presence in schools and preservice teacher-preparation programs catalyzes better educational outcomes. However, sophisticated computers and telecommunications do have unique capabilities for enhancing learning, especially through a new model of education called "distributed learning" in which classrooms, workplaces, homes, and community settings are linked for educational activities. Innovations such as "groupware"— software programs that allow shared database access, electronic meetings, collective writing, etc.—let students in different locations take part in guided, collaborative, inquiry-based learning. This technology eliminates a traditional, offline impediment to collaboration: the need for students and teachers to get together in one place at the same time.

Such experiences have other advantages, which include:

- centering the curriculum on "authentic" problems parallel to those adults face in real-world settings;
- facilitating guided, reflective inquiry through extended projects that teach sophisticated concepts and skills, and result in complex products;
- utilizing computer modeling and visualization as a powerful bridge between experience and abstraction;
- enhancing students' collaboration as they construct meaning through an exchange of perspectives on shared experiences;
- letting pupils partner with teachers to develop learning experiences;
- fostering success for all students through special measures to aid the disabled and the disenfranchised.

To reap these many benefits, however, requires a complex implementation process that includes sustained, large-scale innovations in virtually all aspects of schooling, including curriculum, pedagogy, assessment, professional development, and administration. Strategies to promote equity and partnerships between schools, businesses, homes, and community are needed. And since educational systems greatly benefit from learning about the failures, as well as the successes, of attempted innovations, a learning community of practitioners, researchers, and policymakers is essential to expand the use of "best practices."

Beyond distributing descriptions of innovations, this community can foster dialogue about their implementation. For example, educators can undertake collaborative annotation of video-based case studies of educational practice that include ancillary information, such as student products and teacher reflections. Teachers find direct knowledge about others' practices much more convincing than conventional forms of research evidence.

Such communities have captured the interest of the National Science Foundation (NSF). Three years ago, NSF launched a series of multidisciplinary studies to examine how sophisticated information technologies can foster Knowledge and Distributed Intelligence (KDI). This initiative was prompted by the fundamental shifts that new interactive media are creating in the process of science. Scientists are moving away from an investigative process based on reading others' research results in journal publications as a means of informing and guiding one's own scholarship. Instead, scientists are engaged in virtual communities for creating, sharing, and mastering knowledge: exchanging real-time data, deliberating alternative interpretations of that information, using "groupware" tools to discuss the meaning of findings and create new conceptual frameworks. NSF calls this process "knowledge networking." The KDI studies are examining these virtual communities for their potential impact both on science learning and on learning in general.

For example, a knowledge network to enhance education reform might consist of teachers, administrators, parents, taxpayers, politicians, teacher trainers, researchers, school board members, and other policymakers—each bringing different perspectives. Through tools for representation, collaboration, and community building, new interactive media can create a framework within which constructive interaction can occur.

Already, some knowledge networks are in place, illustrating the range of purposes, designs, and outcomes these virtual communities of practice can accommodate:

- Swarthmore College's Math Forum offers a wide variety of resources and opportunities for communication among mathematical educators, parents and students (**forum.swarthmore.edu**).
- The Teacher Professional Development Institute (TAPPED IN) is a "virtual conference center" that provides educators with the opportunities to access and discuss exemplary reform-based models and

materials; co-construct, review, and publish resources; and actively seek out innovative solutions and exemplary practices in education (**www.tappedin.org**).

- trAce is an online community for writers and readers across the world; participants post their writings, critique each other's work, and discuss their favorite literature, leading to conceptual frameworks for deeper understanding (**trace.ntu.ac.uk/about/about.htm**).
- The World Bank Development Forum is an electronic venue for exchanges on issues of sustainable development among members of the development community (**www.worldbank.org/devforum/**).

As participants gain experience with new interactive media, design strategies for educational knowledge networks are continually improving. Typically, when islands of innovation in education emerge, they do not last, because turning small-scale innovations into widespread changes in standard practices requires shifts in organizational structures, individual beliefs and values, and community commitment. Traditional strategies for transferring innovations from research to practice need to change away from transmitting recipes for innovation. Instead, in virtual communities of practice, researchers and practitioners become co-developers of innovative models. By building bridges from reflective innovation to standard practice, knowledge networks provide an excellent venue for exploring whether such changes may be adapted to and sustained in schools.

The fundamental issue is not whether new instructional tools are more efficient at accomplishing current goals with conventional methods, but instead how emerging media can provide an effective means of reaching essential educational objectives in the technology-driven, knowledge-based economy of this new century. Since computers and telecommunications increasingly enable students and teachers to have rich interactions with resources outside of classroom walls, the mission of schooling is inevitably changing, too.

Commentary by Larry Cuban

"Is being a good citizen only about being a worker and consumer?"

How might we expect the roles of schools to change in our increasingly technological society? We asked Larry Cuban, professor of education at Stanford University, to respond.

Since the late 19th century, the U.S. has been a technological society. The industrialization of the work force, the application of electricity, telegraph, and telephone to business and daily life accelerated the pace of American life well before the automobile and, later, planes became commonplace. Today, with embedded chips in most machines we use daily, we continue to live in a technological society. What distinguishes that earlier period from the one in which we now live is not the technology; it is that the democratic purposes of public schools have been forgotten in the last two decades.

There was no golden age of public schooling a century ago. Racially segregated schools, immigrant children stripped of their native cultures, poor children working in factories, and other characteristics of typical turn-of-the-century life make those decades unappealing times. But in those bygone years the primary purpose of U.S. public schools, beyond the basic task of making the young literate, was building citizens. Americans wholeheartedly endorsed the public school because this unique institution promoted what was then viewed as the common good.

No more, however. In the last two decades a new generation of school reformers has drafted public schools into fighting global economic wars. Economic competition has led in a straight line to national goals for schools, higher academic standards, and raising test scores. Providing marketable skills to students entering an information-driven workplace has completely overwhelmed the purpose of tax-supported public schools building a just democracy.

Other economically driven reformers have rejected public schools and called for more individual parental choice through government-funded vouchers to send children to private schools, independent charter schools, and public schools contracted out to private entrepreneurs. To these reformers, private sector management is the model for public school systems. School and district activities are "downsized," "restructured," and "outsourced." Is being a good citizen only about being a worker and consumer making individual choices of products? I don't think so.

The historic commitment to public schooling in building bonds between diverse groups and nurturing democratic attitudes and behaviors seldom gets a passing nod from techno-enthusiasts or reformers bent on turning schools into places where individual preferences trump the social benefits of schooling.

Because U.S. society has been technological and will continue to be, the issue is how to restrike a better balance than now exists among competing purposes of public schools. It is now time to voice deep concern over the missing democratic purposes that U.S. schools have always served in this society.

Perhaps the furor over the digital divide will drive home the magnitude of the imbalance among purposes for public schooling in a democracy. The digital divide has become a symbol of the social inequities in the larger society; it is about the poor as outsiders to the democratic process and full citizenship. Linking the social inequities that exist in the larger society to the gap in Internet access between poor and wealthy schoolchildren is another way of connecting to the larger social purposes of public schooling. For those who share this concern over Americans forgetting the essential civic role schools perform in our society, more voices need to be raised about the democratic purposes that our schools must serve in a technologically driven society that has, for now, elevated individual greed into a virtue.

Commentary by David Williamson Shaffer

"This is Dewey's vision revisited"

HEL asked David Williamson Shaffer—a lecturer at the Harvard Graduate School of Education, instructor at Harvard Medical School, and acting director of education at the Center for Innovative Minimally Invasive Therapy at the Massachusetts General Hospital—to weigh in on the future of schools in the digital age.

The modern structure of U.S. schools dates back to the Industrial Revolution in the middle of 19th century, when the job of schools was to prepare students to be productive members of an industrial society. Fixed class periods marked by bells, repetition, and rote memorization were excellent preparation for factory life. We have inherited industrial schools, but the Information Revolution is transforming our economy from manufacturing to services—and changing us from a society of factory workers to a society of knowledge workers.

From the perspective of the year 2000, it is hard to predict how technology will change U.S. education: the technology is too new and the potential for change too great. However, it seems likely that education in a knowledge economy will come to resemble work in a knowledge economy—just as education in an industrial economy reflected industrial work.

This probably means that teachers will *not* disappear and leave children to learn from machines. A knowledge economy is built on the value that people create through innovative thinking. Knowledgeable adults will almost certainly continue to play a role in children's development, and that role will continue to involve substantial face-to-face contact, particularly for young children.

However, knowledge workers do learn in ways that differ from traditional K-12 classrooms. Professionals such as lawyers, doctors, architects, engineers, social workers, and educators spend time in formal coursework. But a critical part of their training is some kind of work experience or practicum, under the guidance of a mentor. Architects work in studio courses, social workers log supervised hours, teachers do practice teaching, graduate students work as teaching assistants, and medicine has developed an elaborate system of internship, residency, and fellowship as clinicians take progressively more responsibility for the care of patients.

Learning to be a knowledge worker, in other words, involves participating—with guidance and support—in meaningful activities. In some ways this is Dewey's vision revisited, with students learning by doing the real work of life with appropriate support from adult mentors. By relying on mentors, practicum-based professional education also involves the community in a richer way than does the traditional closed classroom, and is far more dispersed and individualized than classroom-based instruction. Certainly there are central facilities, but the expectation is that a significant part of the learning experience will not be in a single classroom with 30 or more students and a single teacher.

In the new knowledge society, adults will continue to play a meaningful role in engaging students. However, the walls—literal and metaphorical—that make up a traditional school will become far more permeable as practitioners from the outside become more involved in the educational process.

Notes on Contributors

George Brackett is a lecturer in education at the Harvard Graduate School of Education. He is also founder and principal of George Brackett Associates, an educational software development firm, and has designed and programmed a number of award-winning programs.

Melissa Burns is a researcher-writer at the Educational Development Center in Newton, MA.

Shelley Chamberlain is coordinator of educational technology for the Lexington (MA) Public Schools.

Milton Chen is executive director of the George Lucas Educational Foundation in San Rafael, CA. He was previously director of the KQED Center for Education and Lifelong Learning (PBS-San Francisco). He has also been a director of research at the Children's Television Workshop in New York and an assistant professor at the Harvard Graduate School of Education.

Larry Cuban is professor of education at Stanford University, where he works with K-12 teachers and administrators as a faculty sponsor for Stanford Teacher Education Program. Before joining Stanford's faculty, he was a high school social studies teacher for 14 years and a school district superintendent for seven. His books include *Tinkering Toward Utopia: Reflections on School Reform*, written with David Tyack.

Chris Dede is professor of education and information technology at George Mason University. He was the editor of the 1998 Association for Supervision and Curriculum Development Yearbook, *Learning with Technology*. He is a member of the U.S. Department of Education's Expert Panel on Technology and will join the Harvard Graduate School of Education faculty in 2000.

Natalie Engler is a Massachusetts-based features writer who covers technology, business, and education.

Alan Feldman is a principal scientist and center director at TERC, an educational research group based in Cambridge, MA. He is senior author of *Network Science, a Decade Later: The Internet and Classroom Learning*. A teacher and principal for many years, his recent research has focused on inquiry-based approaches to teaching and learning, and the ways that technology can support these approaches.

Wambui Githiora-Updike teaches literature at Emerson College in Boston. Born and raised in Kenya, she has worked on educational radio programs in Uganda and Malawi and has developed multicultural curricula for use in Boston public schools. She holds degrees from the University of Nairobi and the University of Kansas, as well as a doctorate in education from Teachers College, Columbia University.

David T. Gordon is the interim editor of the *Harvard Education Letter*. He has taught writing in Emerson College's School of the Arts and worked as a staff editor for *Newsweek*, writing about foreign affairs, culture, technology, and education.

Howard Gardner is the John H. and Elisabeth A. Hobbs Professor in Cognition and Education at the Harvard Graduate School of Education and a co-director of Project Zero. He is best known in educational circles for his theory of multiple intelligences, a critique of the notion that there exists but a single human intelligence that can be assessed by standard psychometric instruments. He is the author of 18 books, most recently *The Disciplined Mind: What All Students Should Understand* and *Intelligence Reframed: Multiple Intelligences for the 21st Century*.

Thomas Hehir is a distinguished scholar at the Educational Development Center in Newton, MA, and a lecturer at Harvard's Graduate School of Education. As director of the U.S. Department of Education's Office of Special Education programs from 1993–1999, he was responsible for federal leadership in implementing the Individuals with Disabilities Education Act.

Karen Kelly is a contributing writer of the *Harvard Education Letter*. She also reports for The Great Lakes Radio Consortium, a public radio network that covers environmental issues. For eight years she produced a nationally syndicated public radio program about education called *The Best of Our Knowledge*. She is based in Ottawa, Ontario.

Glenn M. Kleiman is a vice president and senior scientist at the Educational Development Center in Newton, MA, where he directs the Center for Online Professional Education and the EdTech Leaders Online project. He is on the faculty of the Harvard Graduate School of Education and the author of *Brave New Schools: How Computers Can Change Education*, as well as numerous articles and chapters on educational technology.

Gene Klotz is Buffington Professor of Mathematics at Swarthmore College and director of the Math Forum, a leading virtual center for mathematics education funded by the National Science Foundation. He was also principal investigator for the NSF-funded project, Visual Geometry: A Multi-Media Approach, which explored three-dimensional geometric concepts using computer animation, video, and workbooks.

Maisie McAdoo is a Brooklyn-based education writer. She has written about education technology for publications such as *Technos, Newsday, Scholastic's Electronic Learning,* and *IEEE Spectrum.* She was a 1996–1997 Fellow in Children and the News at Columbia Graduate School of Journalism, where she researched K-12 reform initiatives in New York City. She is currently an editor at Reuters.

Edward Miller is an education policy analyst and writer, and a former editor of the *Harvard Education Letter.*

Andrea Oseas is assistant director of the Technology in Education program at the Harvard Graduate School of Education.

David Perkins is co-director of Harvard's Project Zero and the author of several books on education. He has conducted research and development in educational technologies; teaching and learning for understanding; and creativity, problem-solving, and reasoning in the arts, sciences, and everyday life. His web-based initiative, Active Learning Practices for Schools, makes Project Zero's resources readily available to schools.

Margaret Riel is associate director of the Center for Collaborative Research in Education at the University of California, Irvine. She is the author of numerous articles on interactive technology and developed Learning Circles, a structured form of global cross-classroom, small-group collaboration now used by the International Education and Resource Network.

David Williamson Shaffer is a lecturer at the Harvard Graduate School of Education, an instructor at Harvard Medical School, and the acting director of education at the Center for Innovative Minimally Invasive Therapy at Massachusetts General Hospital. He holds a Ph.D. in new media and learning from the Media Lab at MIT.

Karen Smith is executive director of TECH CORPS, a national nonprofit that rallies volunteers and corporations to assist K-12 schools with technology equipment and training.

Bill Tally is senior research associate at the Center for Children and Technology in New York City. His main interest is in whether and how new technologies, combined with active-learning pedagogies, can support deeper understanding in and across the disciplines. He has been designing and studying educational applications of new technologies for more than 15 years.

Clorinda Valenti is an education writer and editor based in Albany, NY. She has worked in higher education and for an education association, and was an English teacher in an independent school. For several years she was the editor of *Education New York: The Independent Journal of Schools and Cultural Affairs in the Empire State*, a publication she helped plan and launch.

Joan Westreich is a clinical social worker and psychotherapist in private practice in Manhattan. She is also a writer and editor who covers a range of subjects, including mental health, education, business, and the arts.

Stone Wiske is director of the Technology in Education Program at the Harvard Graduate School of Education. Her recent work focuses on the development and analysis of an online learning environment for educators to support teaching for understanding with new technologies. She is also co-founder of a new journal called *Education, Communication and Information*, to be launched in 2000.

Julie M. Wood, lecturer at the Harvard Graduate School of Education, has a background in elementary education as a teacher and reading consultant, and as a developer of educational products. She co-founded a summer literacy institute for struggling readers/writers in an underserved charter school in Dorchester, MA. She directs the America Reads program at MIT, training undergraduates to work as literacy tutors in inner-city schools.

Who We Are

The *Harvard Education Letter* reports, interprets, and critiques new research and innovative practice in K-12 education. Our mission is to publish accurate, thought-provoking articles in a concise, jargon-free style. Founded in 1985 and published bimonthly by the Harvard Graduate School of Education, the *Letter* is read by more than 60,000 school administrators, teachers, policy-makers, university faculty, and other educators.

Each eight-page issue of the *Harvard Education Letter* covers one or more timely topics in depth, exploring issues from multiple perspectives of research and practice and including lists of helpful resources.

We thank the Spencer Foundation for its continued support of the *Harvard Education Letter,* and of our mission.

Harvard Education Letter Staff

Editorial Director: Kelly Graves-Desai
Interim Editor: David T. Gordon
Editorial Assistant: Izumi Doi
Web Manager: Joan Razzante
Production Editor: Dody Riggs

Faculty Editor

Richard F. Elmore, Professor, Harvard Graduate School of Education

Editorial Advisory Board

Milli Blackman, Director, The Principals' Center, Harvard Graduate School of Education

Linda Darling-Hammond, Professor, Stanford University

Sally Dias, Superintendent, Watertown Public Schools, Watertown, MA

Harold Howe II, Senior Lecturer Emeritus, Harvard Graduate School of Education

Susan Moore Johnson, Professor, Harvard Graduate School of Education

Robert Kegan, Senior Lecturer, Harvard Graduate School of Education

Peggy Kemp, Office of School Partnerships, Harvard Graduate School of Education

Marya Levenson, Superintendent, North Colonie Central School District, Newtonville, NY

Deborah Meier, Head, Mission Hill School, Boston, MA

John Merrow, President, The Merrow Report

Jerome T. Murphy, Professor and Dean, Harvard Graduate School of Education

Arthur J. Rosenthal, Publishing Consultant

Catherine Snow, Professor, Harvard Graduate School of Education

Jay Sugarman, Teacher, Runkle School, Brookline, MA

Ariadne Valsamis, Director of Public Information, Harvard Graduate School of Education

For More Information

Harvard Education Letter
Gutman Library 349
6 Appian Way
Cambridge, MA 02138
Phone: 1-800-513-0763; Outside U.S.: 617-495-3432
Fax: 617-496-3584
Web site: www.edletter.org
Email: Customer service, orders@edletter.org
            Editorial comments, editor@edletter.org